THE FACTS ABOUT CORONARY BYPASS SURGERY

Did you know:

• An estimated 350,000 coronary bypass operations will be performed this year.

• You can dramatically reduce the chance of developing coronary artery disease by learning the seven most avoidable risk factors—and doing something about them.

• The benefits of bypass surgery may last indefinitely, yet you may require reoperation unless you adopt a heart-healthy life-style.

• Bypass surgery is still controversial, but three tests, described in this book, can determine unquestionably if it is required.

The facts can save your life. They're all here, plus questions to ask and answers you must have before making an educated decision about . . .

CORONARY BYPASS SURGERY

THE DELL SURGICAL LIBRARY:

DELL SURGICAL LIBRARY

THE WELL-INFORMED PATIENT'S GUIDE TO

CORONARY BYPASS SURGERY

JEFFREY P. GOLD, M.D., AND TONY EPRILE

A DELL BOOK

Published by
Dell Publishing
a division of
Bantam Doubleday Dell Publishing Group, Inc.
666 Fifth Avenue
New York, New York 10103

This book is not intended as a substitute for medical advice of physicians and should be used only in conjunction with the advice of your personal doctor. The reader should regularly consult a physician in matters relating to his or her health and particularly in respect of any symptoms which may require diagnosis or medical attention.

Published by arrangement with G. S. Sharpe Communications, Inc., 606 West 116 Street, New York, New York 10027

ISBN: 0-440-20711-8

Printed in the United States of America

Published simultaneously in Canada

April 1991

10 9 8 7 6 5 4 3 2 1

OPM

Contents

Introduction

The coronary artery bypass operation is rapidly becoming one of America's most common major surgical procedures, with an estimated 350,000 to be performed this year. This is all the more remarkable, given the relative newness of the operation—the first one was done by Dr. René Favaloro at the Cleveland Clinic in 1967. A mere twenty years ago open-heart surgery was regarded as the medical equivalent of men walking on the moon. Today, such surgery has become commonplace.

This medical revolution has been made possible by great strides both in the available technology and in the surgeons' own technique. Patients survive bypass surgery so well that its mortality rate is better than that of gallbladder operations and close to that of tonsillectomies. The list of bypass patients reads like a *Who's Who* of politics and entertainment: including two former secretaries of state, Henry Kissinger and Alexander M. Haig; cohost of the *The MacNeil-Lehrer Newshour* Jim

Lehrer; and the radio talk-show host Larry King (who in fact wrote a book about his own operation). The procedure has already found its way into serious literature as well. In *The Counterlife*, a novel by Philip Roth that was a National Book Award finalist, a forty-year-old dentist's struggle over whether to undergo bypass surgery in the hope that it will improve his sex life is a major part of the plot.

The almost celebrity status of this operation has its flip side, however. Some critics assert that many coronary bypass operations are being done that are not warranted medically. These critics, including both physicians and laymen, have questioned whether the bypass operation improves the longevity of its recipients nearly as much as its advocates have claimed. Some go even farther than that. In a recent *New York Times* article former secretary of health, education, and welfare Joseph A. Califano, Jr., wrote: "There is growing consensus that half the coronary bypasses . . . are unnecessary."

Amid this climate of controversy, people who have had the operation or are considering having it can justifiably feel confused. On the one hand are the increasingly vocal critics of what has become a $5 billion-per-year industry. On the other hand are their own doctors telling them that their lives may be at risk if they don't have the operation. Most men over age fifty will have one or more friends who have undergone bypass. The majority of these people are likely to say how much their health has benefited from the operation, but a small portion of them will complain of depression and continuing symptoms.

The medical literature is not much help either. A brief search will reveal numerous books and articles supporting the conclusion that the coronary artery bypass operation does save lives, increase longevity, and improve the quality of life. The same search may well unearth other studies that say that some cardiac patients can expect just as long and productive a life if treated through less intrusive means, such as medical maintenance.

One problem is that meaningful comparisons between surgically treated and medically treated population groups are hard to come by. Clearly, this is not a situation where it is possible to do double-blind studies (in which neither the doctor nor the patient knows what course of treatment is being pursued). It is even difficult to be sure that like population groups are being compared, because it would be unethical for doctors not to encourage the patients with more advanced coronary artery disease to have the operation. Even the cross-cultural studies—such as that which demonstrated that Americans have the same death rate from heart disease as the British while receiving bypass operations six times as often—are subject to interpretation. Similar studies show English-speaking nations to lead the rest of the world in deaths from heart disease, yet no one would suggest that speaking English raises the risk of a heart attack.

One of the strongest studies to support the value of bypass operations for a broad range of patients appeared in the *Journal of the American Medical Association (JAMA)* in April 1989. Providing a fifteen-year perspective on 5,809 patients, the study (conducted at Duke University) "demonstrates a significant improvement in patient survival with contemporary surgical therapy for the majority of patients with ischemic heart disease."

The *JAMA* report points out one reason why some of

the earlier studies were inconclusive: the operation has been evolving every year, and therefore any long-term study needs to adjust for the progressive improvement in the survival rate each year if the statistics are to be meaningful today. In other words, bypass operations performed ten years ago may not have significantly improved a patient's longevity when compared with medical treatment. Bypass operations performed five years ago—and to an even greater extent those done today—do significantly increase patients' life span.

You should not let yourself be overly alarmed by negative statements such as that of Joseph Califano, Jr. The critics' complaints about the frequency of bypass operations provide a useful caution against American medicine's tendency to overuse the technical fix, but they do a disservice as well. Not mentioned in Mr. Califano's conclusion is the fact that there are situations in which even the operation's fiercest opponents would agree that a coronary bypass is the treatment of choice. The improvement in the *quality* of life for most patients with symptoms of angina is another issue about which there is no question. And finally, it is a mistake to declare an operation "unnecessary" because absolute proof that it will prolong life in a particular situation cannot be obtained. There are simply no hundred-percent guarantees in medicine.

One returns to an important truism in modern medicine: the need to treat the patient, not just the disease. For each patient, bypass surgery is a major operation and one of the most significant events in that person's lifetime . . . regardless of statistics about how widespread the operation and low the mortality rate. Each case of heart disease needs to be examined on its individual merits, with the patient playing an active role in the decision-making process. The better informed the patient and the more he or she is involved in the choice of treatment, the more likely it is that person will be happy with the outcome.

Knowing what to expect helps to alleviate much of the fear associated with any major operation and can prevent the depression experienced by about one sixth of all bypass patients. The well-informed patient is a boon to the doctor as well, since even the decision to try treatment with medication and means other than bypass surgery requires that the personality and life-style of the patient be taken into account.

The decision to go ahead with major surgery is never an easy one, and you are bound to have some anxiety about the prospect. If your health condition warrants bypass surgery, you may wish to bear in mind the words of one patient who found his life vastly enhanced by the procedure: "It shouldn't be called a bypass. It's a forward pass!"

The goal of this book is to give you the information you will need to be a more effective patient and a more active participant in this major decision about your own health. We will examine the conditions that lead to coronary artery disease, how to determine whether bypass would be useful in your case, the bypass operation itself, its aftereffects (both good and bad), the pros and cons of alternative treatments, what you should do to maintain your cardiac health *after* the operation, and how to choose the doctors and hospital best suited to your needs.

CHAPTER 1

Who Gets Coronary Disease and Why

Tom had gone to his doctor for a routine physical checkup as part of the requirements before beginning a new job, and he expected the visit to be just that: routine. Tom, a fifty-two-year-old accountant, was surprised when his physician recommended that he go for an exercise tolerance test (also known as a stress electrocardiogram), urging that he do so sooner rather than later. He had never suffered anything more serious than a twenty-four-hour flu, and although he would be the first to admit that he could stand to lose a few pounds and wasn't nearly as fit as in his college days, he had never experienced chest pain or shortness of breath. (Well, maybe a little when playing tennis on his last vacation. . . .) Anyway, he was much too young for heart disease. He wondered whether the further testing suggested by his doctor was not just a waste of money.

For the physician, Tom presented a completely different picture: that of someone who was clearly a candidate for coronary artery disease and possibly at risk of a sudden heart attack. Before beginning the physical examination the doctor had questioned Tom closely about his life-style habits and about any history of illness in his family. In this case, the history revealed that Tom smoked close to a pack of cigarettes a day and that his father had died at the age of sixty of a coronary. He also expressed some frustration with his career, which was stressful yet had not completely fulfilled his ambition. The physical examination showed that Tom was a full twenty pounds overweight and had elevated blood pressure and cholesterol levels. With the exception of diabetes, he fit all of the risk factors that have come to be associated with cardiovascular illness (disorders of the heart and blood vessels). That Tom did not have chest pain or other symptoms was a good sign, but it by no means put him in the clear.

The condition that leads to coronary artery disease is known as *atherosclerosis*, hardening and clogging of the arteries by fatty plaque, or *atheromas*. The buildup of this plaque can reduce the flow of oxygenated blood to the body's cells, starving them of needed fuel and impairing their very function. This is particularly serious when the clogged artery is one that supplies the heart's own muscles with the oxygen necessary to enable the heart to send oxygenated blood throughout the body.

Besides reduced blood flow, an additional danger of atherosclerosis is that a portion of the plaque may break off and completely obstruct the artery. Should this occur in the heart or the brain, it can be fatal. Constricted arteries present yet another risk: that a weakened section of the diseased artery may rupture, resulting in bleeding (hemorrhage). If this occurs in the brain, a stroke results.

The factors that increase the likelihood of atherosclerosis in the coronary arteries can be usefully divided into those that are avoidable or treatable and those that cannot be controlled. The major avoidable or treatable risk factors are cigarette smoking, high blood-cholesterol levels, high blood pressure, and diabetes. Other possible risk factors include obesity, a sedentary life-style, and certain personality characteristics. Of these, high cholesterol, smoking, and high blood pressure are considered to be primary risk factors; the others are secondary, or contributory. The unavoidable risk factors are age, gender (men are at considerably greater risk than women), and heredity, especially if a parent or sibling suffered a heart attack or sudden death before the age of fifty.

Evidence that these factors raise the risk of a heart attack was first confirmed in one of the most extensive epidemiological studies of this century, the Framingham Heart Study. Named after the Massachusetts town in which it was conducted, the Framingham study is now more than forty years old. During that time some five thousand Framingham residents, representing all ages and a cross-section of the community, have been followed medically by a team of researchers from Harvard and Boston universities in conjunction with the National Institutes of Health. In the beginning, the study participants did not have overt signs of heart disease. Each was interviewed about diet and life-style habits and was given an extensive physical examination, with a follow-up every two years since then. When any participant in the study died, the researchers conducted their own postmortem to determine the exact cause of death. The Framingham study has shown that individuals who exhibited one or more of the risk factors were both more likely to develop coronary artery disease and more likely to do so at an earlier stage than people who did not share the risk factors. And the more risk factors any single individual had, the greater the likelihood of a heart attack.

"I already have heart disease according to my doctor, so what does it matter how I got where I am?" you may ask. One reason to be aware of the risk factors is that correcting them can help prevent further occlusion of your arteries and may even reduce some of the obstruction. This is important regardless of whether you will be treated medically or with surgery. Neither approach cures heart disease. A bypass operation merely sets the illness back to an earlier and less acute stage, while medication can relieve symptoms, but also does not "cure" atherosclerosis. Thus you should avoid habits that might exacerbate the condition.

AVOIDABLE RISK FACTORS

High Cholesterol

Cholesterol is a fat-ester in a family of substances called lipids. It circulates in the blood and is also found in every cell in the body. It is necessary to life, since it is essential to a number of vital processes, including the building of cell walls, the production of steroid and sex hormones, and the manufacture of vitamin D, among others. Problems occur, however, when too much cholesterol is present in the bloodstream. Then fatty streaks start to form on the inside of the artery walls and these eventually form the basis for the plaque that can interfere with effective blood flow and is the main cause of coronary heart disease.

Cholesterol metabolism and circulation are complex processes with considerable variation among individuals. Both diet and heredity play a role in determining whether you will develop high blood cholesterol. Some people have an inherited tendency to manufacture excessive cholesterol, and if their diet is high in saturated fats, cholesterol, and total calories, they are likely to develop high blood levels. (It is important to distinguish between dietary cholesterol, which is found in animal products, and blood cholesterol, which is what circulates in your blood. When your doctor refers to high cholesterol, it is the latter that is of concern, although dietary cholesterol also plays a role in developing high blood levels.) About three fifths of the body's cholesterol is manufactured by the liver, which regulates its output according to the amount of cholesterol in the blood. The remainder of the cholesterol is absorbed through the bowel from food containing cholesterol. However, a diet high in fats, cholesterol, and total calories has the insidious effect of upsetting the liver's regulatory mechanism and overburdening the receptors that remove cholesterol-carrying proteins from the blood.

Doctors agree that anyone with high blood-cholesterol levels—and especially someone with suspected or diagnosed coronary artery disease—should make every attempt to lower it. Until recently, however, there was no clear agreement as to what constituted high cholesterol and how it should be treated. In late 1988, the National Cholesterol Education Program, a nationwide effort coordinated by the National Institutes of Health, released guidelines covering all adults and providing specific recommendations for diagnosis and treatment.

Total cholesterol levels are measured in terms of milligrams per deciliter of blood (mg/dL), and the level considered acceptable has been steadily revised downward over the last twenty years. Under the National Cholesterol Education Program guidelines, a blood cholesterol level of 200 mg/dL or less is defined as desirable, requiring no further action other than a repeat measurement every five years. Readings in the 200-to-239-mg/dL range are borderline or high, depending upon whether you have other risk factors. In either event you should have another cholesterol measurement to confirm that you do, indeed, fall in this range. If subsequent tests confirm that you do, then the approach to treatment depends upon whether or not you also have two or more other cardiovascular risk factors (see list in Table 1). If you do not, then the treatment consists of dietary changes and education.

If you have two other risk factors, or if your total blood cholesterol is above 240 mg/dL, you fall into a high-risk group. As a first step, the National Cholesterol Education Program recommends a lipoprotein analysis. As noted earlier, cholesterol is a fatlike substance, and as with any fat, it does not mix with water. The blood is mostly water, so in order for cholesterol to travel through the bloodstream, it must be attached to something that can, namely, a lipoprotein, which is a lipid-carrying protein. Lipoproteins come in different weights and sizes, and some are more instrumental in atherosclerosis than others.

The major classes of lipoproteins are:

- *Very low density lipoproteins (VLDL)*, which carry a combination of cholesterol and triglycerides. Triglycerides are the most abundant of the lipids. While their precise role in atherosclerosis has not been established, high levels of triglycerides are considered an indication of potential problems.

- *Low density lipoproteins (LDL)*, which contain cholesterol and a protein called apolipoprotein B. High levels of LDL cholesterol (defined as 130 mg/dL or more) are considered detrimental because LDLs adhere to the arterial walls, and thus are instrumental in atherosclerosis.

- *High density lipoproteins (HDL)*, which also carry cholesterol, but are considered beneficial because they transport it away from the arterial walls and also are instrumental in clearing excessive amounts from the body.

In recent years, much has appeared in the popular press about the good HDL cholesterol versus the bad LDL cholesterol. Unfortunately, many people have the mistaken notion that if their HDL levels are high, they needn't worry about the total cholesterol. This is not true. As noted by Dr. DeWitt Goodman, panel chairman of the National Cholesterol Education Program, high HDL levels may have some protective effect, but if your total cholesterol is above 240 mg/dL, you should make every effort to lower it, even if you have favorable HDL levels.

A number of scientific studies have confirmed the benefits of reducing high blood cholesterol. For example, the Lipid Research Clinics Coronary Primary Prevention Trials compared a large number of middle-aged men with high cholesterol levels who were being treated with cholesterol-lowering drugs with similar patients being treated with placebos or no drugs. The drugs lowered the patients' cholesterol by 8.5 percent, but what was even more significant is that this group experienced 19 percent fewer deaths from coronary attacks. In other words, for each 1 percent reduction in cholesterol levels, there was a 2 percent reduction in heart attacks and sudden death. The conclusion from this and other studies is that even a slight lowering of overall cholesterol levels has a significant beneficial effect on coronary artery disease and patient life span.

Diet is the primary treatment for high blood cholesterol. This entails reducing intake of fat, especially saturated fats which raise blood cholesterol, and dietary cholesterol. Losing excessive weight also lowers cholesterol. Certain medications, such as birth control pills, may raise cholesterol. The use of anabolic steroids—especially by young athletes seeking to increase muscle mass—has a disastrous effect on cholesterol by lowering HDLs to extraordinarily low levels. Regular exercise tends to increase HDLs and may help lower total cholesterol, especially if it is part of a weight-reduction program.

If these dietary measures fail to bring your cholesterol down to desirable levels, then you may be put on a cholesterol-lowering medication. (See Chapter Nine.) Drug therapy may be especially important for people with a relatively unusual genetic disorder called familial hypercholesterolemia. People with this condition have very high cholesterol levels that can lead to extensive heart disease at an early age if not treated. Careful monitoring by both physician and patient, combined with aggressive medical therapy, can keep this disease in check. New developments in cholesterol-reducing drugs that have few side effects should allow patients with hypercholesterolemia to control their cholesterol levels while leading normal lives.

Cigarette Smoking

Most people are aware that cigarettes increase the risk of emphysema and lung cancer, but many do not realize that cigarette use is also the leading cause of premature death from heart attacks in the United States. The latest Surgeon General's Report on Smoking and Health estimates that more than 350,000 preventable heart attack deaths each year are directly related to smoking. And if you have other cardiovascular risk factors, such as high blood pressure or high cholesterol, your risk may be four- or five-fold greater than it would be if you did not smoke. The good news is that stopping smoking very quickly has a beneficial effect, and within three to five years of quitting, a smoker's risk of a heart attack is about the same as that of a nonsmoker with a similar risk-factor profile.

Specific harmful cardiovascular effects of smoking have been enumerated by the American Heart Association as follows:

- Decreasing the amount of available oxygen carried by the blood, thus increasing the work the heart has to do to provide oxygen to every cell.
- Lowering the amount of HDL, the lipoprotein that helps to remove excess cholesterol from the bloodstream. (See above.)
- Affecting the mechanisms that control blood pressure.

- Introducing substances to the bloodstream that attack the inner lining of the arteries, causing scarring and increased buildup of plaque.
- Affecting the clot-control mechanisms, thus increasing the risk that dangerous blood clots will form.

Carbon monoxide, which makes up one to five percent of cigarette smoke, is the major culprit. The amount of available oxygen carried in the blood is reduced because the carbon monoxide binds with hemoglobin at the receptor sites that would otherwise bind with oxygen. Carbon monoxide also causes hemoglobin to bind more tightly with oxygen, thus making it more difficult for the body's cells to extract the oxygen they need.

Doctors suspect that the excess carbon monoxide carried in the bloodstream upsets the delicate balance of a variety of other processes, including the mechanisms controlling clotting. In addition, carbon monoxide causes arteries to constrict, thus increasing blood pressure (much the way water pressure is increased when you squeeze the end of a hosepipe). The net effect is that the heart has to work harder to supply oxygen to the rest of the body, at the same time that its own supply of oxygen is reduced.

It should be noted that smoke from low-tar cigarettes has a higher percentage of carbon monoxide than that from regular cigarettes, and that smokers tend to draw harder on the low-yield cigarettes and inhale more smoke. There are therefore no cardiac health benefits to switching to a low-yield brand, despite any implications made by advertisers of such products.

The means by which smoking accelerates atherosclerosis is not completely understood, although the epidemiological evidence clearly demonstrates that it does so.

One theory holds that smoking increases the number of oxygen free radicals in the bloodstream. These are molecules that are unstable because they lack an electron. They are important catalysts in many metabolic functions, but they can also be destructive. Free radicals alter the chemistry of the molecules with which they come into contact in two ways: either by "stealing" electrons to make up for the ones they are missing or by giving up an extra electron to the other molecules. In the body, free radicals react with proteins and, more significantly, with the fatty acids in cell membranes. It is thought that oxygen free radicals might damage the arterial walls by making the cells that line them more accessible to LDL cholesterol and/or by directly injuring the tissue, which then becomes scarred and thickened by the immune system's own defenses against injury.

Another way smoking promotes the formation of plaque is by changing the way that blood clots form. Since a marked reduction in plaque can occur in as short a period as six months to a year after a smoker completely quits the habit, it is possible that much of the increased clogging of arteries among smokers can be attributed to this cause.

Smokers have also been found to have lower HDL levels than nonsmokers. Why this is so is not clear, but it indicates that smoking is a double-edged sword that not only damages the arteries and the heart but also significantly *exacerbates* the damage caused by other risk factors.

High Blood Pressure (Hypertension)

Blood pressure is the amount of force that the blood exerts on the walls of the arteries as it flows through the circulatory system. The rate and pressure of the blood flow is continuously fine-tuned by the body according to the needs of various organs and the stresses with which the body must cope. Unfortunately, for some sixty million Americans, the tuning is slightly out of whack and their blood pressure is consistently higher than it should be. This hypertension is damaging to the entire cardiovascular system, forcing the heart to work harder to provide blood to all the body's cells and reducing the blood vessels' elasticity by constant strain (much the way overinflation increases the wear and tear on an automobile tire).

The increased pressure also makes it likely that any weakened areas in the arterial walls (aneurysms) will balloon out and interfere with surrounding nerve and cell function, create a pocket of turbulence where dangerous blood clots can form, or give way and allow blood to hemorrhage into surrounding tissue.

Blood pressure is measured in millimeters of mercury, abbreviated as mm/Hg, or Torr and expressed in two numbers, such as 120/80 mm/Hg. The first or large number represents the *systolic* pressure, which occurs immediately following the heartbeat (contraction). The smaller number represents the *diastolic* pressure, which occurs when the heart is resting momentarily between beats.

During the course of a day, your blood pressure varies considerably. It is lowest in the early morning hours while you are asleep, and begins to rise before dawn. It may go up to very high levels during exercise or periods of stress. These temporary fluctuations are not important; what counts is your average blood pressure while sitting quietly. The National High Blood Pressure Education Program defines normal adult blood pressure as below 140/85, with 120/80–70 considered ideal. (See Table 2.) To establish a diagnosis of high blood pressure, several readings taken on different occasions should be used. If the *average* is above normal, steps should be taken to lower it. The most reliable readings still come from the standard manual *sphygmomanometer* (pronounced sfig-mo-mon-OM-et-er), the familiar instrument with an inflatable cuff and column of mercury or other measuring device. Automatic devices such as the "digitalized" monitors that slip over a finger or wrist are notoriously subject to error. Home monitoring devices can be useful in some circumstances, but the machines should be calibrated with your doctor's to make sure the readings are similar.

Over the years, insurance statistics have correlated an increase in mortality with each increase in blood pressure, and high blood pressure is often referred to as "the silent killer" because a person can have high blood pressure for many years without experiencing overt symptoms. Once diagnosed, mild to moderate hypertension is usually treated with a trial of nondrug therapies for several months. These include reducing salt intake, losing excess weight, increasing exercise, stopping smoking, and cutting down on excessive alcohol use. If these life-style changes fail to lower blood pressure sufficiently, antihypertensive drugs will be added to the regimen.

In about five to ten percent of the cases, the hypertension is the direct result of a physical disorder—such as certain kidney problems or tumors of the adrenal glands—or a response to existing medication, such as oral contraceptives. In the majority of cases, however, there is no obvious cause—this is referred to as primary or essential hypertension. Heredity may be the principal factor, and life-style certainly plays a part . . . but much less so than commonly supposed.

For the majority of people, hypertension can be

controlled but not "cured." Many different types of blood-pressure-lowering drugs are now available. Often, a single pill a day will suffice; in others, a combination of drugs may be needed. But almost all cases of high blood pressure can now be controlled with minimal side-effects. Early detection and frequent monitoring to make sure that the levels are in the normal range go a long way to minimizing arterial damage and reducing the risk of stroke, heart attack, and kidney damage—three of the most common consequences of untreated high blood pressure.

Diabetes

Diabetes is a complex metabolic disorder in which the body is unable to properly metabolize food, especially carbohydrates. As a result, too much glucose (blood sugar) circulates in the bloodstream and may "spill over" into the urine. There are two types of diabetes: juvenile onset or Type I, which is characterized by a lack of the hormone insulin; and adult onset or Type II, in which the body produces insulin but is unable to produce enough or use it effectively. This can also be classified as insulin dependent diabetes mellitus (IDDM) and non-insulin dependent diabetes mellitus (NIDDM).

People with diabetes have a greatly increased incidence of atherosclerosis, heart attacks, and high blood pressure. In fact, about half of all diabetics die prematurely from coronary artery disease, and another twenty-five percent die from other vascular disorders. Good control of blood sugar levels is imperative to prevent early complications from this disease, especially for people suffering from Type I diabetes. Because diabetes already increases the risk of heart disease, diabetic patients should be particularly careful to control and minimize the other risk factors.

Obesity

People who are twenty percent or more above their desirable weight have an increased incidence of heart attacks. This may be due to the fact that overweight people tend to have high blood cholesterol. High blood pressure also is more common among overweight people. Even so, recent statistics from the Framingham Heart Study indicate that obesity may also be an independent risk factor for a heart attack.

Anyone who is overweight and has heart disease should lose the excess weight, but crash or fad diets should be avoided. The best way to lose weight, and then keep it off, is to alter your eating habits to decrease total calories and fat intake. (Remember, a gram of fat has nine calories, more than twice the four calories in a gram of carbohydrate or protein.) Many people overlook the calories in beverages. Alcohol contains seven calories per gram, and soft drinks, juices, wine, and beer all are sources of calories. In addition to cutting back on calories (you should consume at least one thousand a day if you are a woman and twelve hundred to fourteen hundred if you are a man) you should increase your physical activity. This will speed the weight loss and also prevents metabolic changes that make it easier to regain the lost pounds.

Sedentary Life-style

"Whenever I feel the urge to exercise, I lie down until the feeling goes away," Mark Twain once said, and people have been echoing this sentiment ever since. Thanks to modern labor-saving devices, automobiles, and other work savers, we can now lead a sedentary life. But this is not in the best interests of good health. Regular moderate exercise bolsters the strength of the heart's own muscle, improves blood flow, raises HDL levels for reasons as yet not fully understood, and may have beneficial effects on the overall immune system, the body's defenses against disease.

A word of caution, however; anyone with heart disease or a high-risk profile should consult a doctor before beginning an exercise conditioning program. An exercise tolerance test is recommended beforehand by anyone over the age of forty who has been relatively sedentary and for even younger people who have heart disease or cardiovascular risk factors.

In devising an exercise program, moderation and regularity are key factors. The exercise need not be strenuous—twenty or thirty minutes of brisk walking three or four times a week (preferably on alternate days) is all that is required. Other excellent aerobic exercises (defined as activities that use large muscles and require increased oxygen that can be maintained for a period of time) include stair climbing, cycling, swimming, jogging (if your knees and other joints can take it), rowing, or cross-country skiing (either with a machine or on snow).

Personality Characteristics and Stress

Stress has long been associated with heart attacks and other illnesses, but the mechanisms involved are unknown. Some researchers think that stress may alter hormonal levels or immune responses, making a person more vulnerable to disease. Others think that it's the way we respond to stress that's important, and this is where personality characteristics come into play.

The Type A personality was first linked with heart disease by two San Francisco–based cardiologists, Drs. Ray Rosenman and Meyer Friedman. They found that people with certain personality characteristics—for example, those that are driven to achieve, extra time-and-deadline conscious, impatient, and hostile, among others—are especially prone to heart disease. But not all Type A characteristics seem to be involved. More recent studies by these and other researchers, including a team at Duke University, have identified hostility, anger, and suspicion as particularly detrimental to the heart. More studies are needed to determine whether excessive hostility and anger do, indeed, increase the risk of a heart attack. In the meantime, many doctors recommend behavior modification for people who exhibit these traits.

UNAVOIDABLE RISK FACTORS

Heredity

Many researchers consider this the most important risk factor of all. Coronary artery disease tends to run in families, and the risk of a heart attack is high among people whose parents or siblings suffered an early heart attack or sudden death. But we are not total victims of our genes. Even if you have an unfavorable family history, you can reduce your risk by minimizing avoidable risk factors, such as smoking.

Prospective bypass patients and their family members who are reading this book should try to have the whole family take part in the move to a healthier lifestyle. This will not only encourage you to maintain your diet and exercise program, but will help the other members of your family protect themselves against any predisposition to heart disease.

Gender

Men are more susceptible to atherosclerosis, probably due to a combination of hormonal makeup and ways of coping with life stresses, than women. However, cardiovascular illness is the number-one killer of women as well as of men, although it usually affects them at a later stage in life. Approximately twenty-eight percent of bypass patients are women. Women who smoke are at higher risk. The incidence of heart disease among women also rises after menopause, when women lose the protective effect of female hormones. Recent studies indicate, however, that estrogen replacement therapy may help protect against heart disease, although this may raise the risk of other diseases, including some types of cancer.

Age

The risk of a heart attack increases with age. As you get older, a certain amount of physical deterioration is inevitable. After menopause women begin to "catch up" with men in developing heart disease. For both sexes the muscles of the heart, and indeed of the body as a whole, begin to lose some of their tone and become less supple, and the arteries lose some of their elasticity. These natural processes can be accelerated or delayed by life-style habits and heredity.

While the aging process cannot be prevented altogether, modern medicine and better understanding of nutrition and health are helping more and more of us to live out our full span of years.

Table 1: Risk status based on presence of CHD risk factors other than LDL-cholesterol

The patient is considered to have a high risk status if he or she has one of the following:

EITHER:

Definite CHD: the characteristic clinical picture and objective laboratory findings of either:

- **Definite prior myocardial infarction**, or
- **Definite myocardial ischemia, such as angina pectoris**

OR:

Two other CHD risk factors:

- **Male sex***
- **Family history of premature CHD** (definite myocardial infarction or sudden death before age 55 in a parent or sibling)
- **Cigarette smoking** (currently smokes more than 10 cigarettes per day)
- **Hypertension**
- **Low HDL-cholesterol concentration** (below 35 mg/dl confirmed by repeat measurement)
- **Diabetes mellitus**
- **History of definite cerebrovascular or occlusive peripheral vascular disease**
- **Severe obesity** ($\geq$ 30% overweight)

*Male sex is considered a risk factor in this scheme because the rates of CHD are 3–4 times higher in men than in women in the middle decades of life and roughly 2 times higher in the elderly. Hence, a man with one other CHD risk factor is considered to have a high risk status, whereas a woman is not so considered unless she has two other CHD risk factors.

SOURCE: National Cholesterol Education Program, National Institutes of Health, 1988.

Table 2: Classification of blood pressure* in adults 18 years or older

Range (mmHg)

DIASTOLIC

Below 85	Normal
85–90	High normal
90–104	Mild hypertension
Above 105	Moderate to severe hypertension

SYSTOLIC

Below 140	Normal
140–159	Mild elevation
Above 160	Moderate to severe elevation

EXAMPLES:

145/95:	Mild hypertension
160/105:	Moderately severe hypertension
175/115:	Severe hypertension

Adapted from the National High Blood Pressure Education Program, 1988.

*Based on the average of two or more readings on two or more occasions.

CHAPTER 2

Understanding the Cardiovascular System

"I knew it was important to be informed about my condition before agreeing to an operation," said Charles, a lawyer in his late sixties and a recent bypass patient, "and my cardiologist was happy to explain everything to me. He even showed me diagrams and X-ray pictures. The only problem was I didn't understand a word he said."

Charles's difficulty in following his cardiologist's explanations is not at all unusual. For many patients, their last encounter with physiological terminology was in the high-school science lab. With the nervousness one naturally feels when being told what might be wrong with one's own body (and, perhaps, a fear that the doctor will consider you ignorant), it is little wonder that many patients simply nod agreement at their briefing sessions and hope for the best.

In this chapter, we provide a brief review of how the heart and circulatory system work, what coronary artery disease is, and an explanation of some of the common terms you will need to know when discussing your condition with a doctor. A glossary is also provided at the back of the book to help you with any unfamiliar terminology. We would recommend that you read through this section at least once to get a general sense of the heart's physiology, and refer to it later as needed.

THE HEART AND CORONARY ARTERY DISEASE

The human heart, a muscular organ about the size of a person's fist, performs a remarkable amount of work during a person's lifetime. At the normal rate of approximately seventy-two beats per minute, or a little over one hundred thousand times in twenty-four hours, the heart circulates the equivalent of approximately two thousand gallons of blood each day. The body's entire blood supply passes through the heart about once every sixty seconds. This circulation is vital to the life of all the cells in our bodies, since it provides them with the oxygen and nutrients that form the energy and building materials they require to perform their tasks. The blood circulation also helps maintain body temperature and carries away the waste products—principally carbon dioxide—from each individual cell.

The muscles of the heart which make all this possible are themselves run on oxygen supplied by blood circulation. Vast quantities of blood pass through the heart every minute, but the heart's own blood supply makes use of only about three to five percent of the total blood supply. Blood is supplied to the heart by the coronary arteries, which surround the heart like a crown or *corona*. The cells of the heart use oxygen more effectively than most cells in the body, and are consequently less able to withstand lengthy periods of oxygen deprivation. If a coronary artery is completely blocked, the heart muscle served by that artery will starve and suffer cell damage, with potentially disastrous effects for the entire circulatory system. The severity of illness caused by such blockages depends both on their extent and on their location, since different parts of the heart have different functions.

The Four Chambers of the Heart and the Two Circulatory Systems

For convenience, one can think of the body as having two related circulatory systems:

The *pulmonary circulation*, which is controlled by the right side of the heart, takes blood that has given up its oxygen to the body's cells and passes it along to the lungs, where the blood exchanges carbon dioxide and other waste products for oxygen.

The *systemic circulation*, which is controlled by the left side of the heart, takes the oxygenated blood from the lungs and sends it coursing throughout the entire body by powerful, wavelike contractions of the left ventricle.

The organ responsible for blood circulation and thus life itself, the heart, is situated slightly left of the center of the chest in front of the lungs, and is held in place by a tough sac of tissue, the *pericardium*. The left and the right sides of the heart are separated by a wall of muscular tissue, the *septum*. Each side of the heart is divided into two chambers, the *atrium* and the *ventricle*, which are linked together by valves. These valves prevent blood from backing up when the muscles relax between beats and ensure that the blood always flows in the right direction.

Oxygenated blood enters the left atrium through the pulmonary veins; the blood then passes through the *mitral valve* into the left ventricle, the largest and most muscular of the heart's chambers. The left ventricle contracts powerfully, sending the oxygenated blood throughout the body's largest artery, the *aorta*, which branches into ever smaller arteries as the blood travels to the rest of the body. It would be unproductive for the left ventricle to expel all the blood it contains each time it contracts, and the percentage of blood that it ejects—called the *ejection fraction*—varies from person to person depending on their sex, age, and physical condition. An athlete might have an ejection fraction of seventy percent; a person whose heart muscle has become damaged from arterial blockage might have an ejection fraction of forty percent or lower. Obviously, the lower the ejection fraction, the less oxygenated blood is being supplied to the body with each heartbeat.

The deoxygenated blood is returned to the heart via the veins, entering the right atrium through two large channels, the *superior* and *inferior vena cava*. The blood then passes through the *tricuspid valve* into the right ventricle, which pumps it through the pulmonary artery into the lungs, where the waste carbon dioxide is exchanged for oxygen. The blood then flows through the pulmonary veins into the left atrium, beginning the cycle again.

The Heart's Electrical System

The heart's ability to pump blood at an even pressure (and to increase or decrease the rate and pressure of blood circulation) is governed by electrical impulses that cause the heart's muscles to constrict in a wavelike motion. Pacemaker cells (located in the sinus node in the right atrium) produce electrical stimulation, which causes a progressive contraction of the *myocardial* (heart muscle) cells as a wave of positive charges advances down the interior of the cells. The contraction of the atria fills the ventricles with blood. The electrical impulse is then delayed and concentrated in the *atrioventricular* node, which acts as a trigger for the electrical impulses that cause the ventricles to contract. As the wave of positive charges that cause contraction recede, the cells repolarize (become negatively charged) and the muscles relax until electrical stimulation starts the process again.

It should be noted that this wavelike motion of the heart muscle is the ideal means of pumping blood under pressure without damaging either the blood cells or the cells with which they come in contact. While machines are now able to take over the heart's pumping duties for brief periods, none have been able to duplicate the beneficial aspects of the rhythmic contraction of the left ventricle. The few hours that the blood is circulated by machine during the coronary bypass operation rarely causes lasting damage, but cardiac surgeons make sure they work fastest during this period to minimize complications.

The Blood Vessels

There are two main kinds of blood vessel: **ARTERIES**, which branch off into smaller blood vessels called *arterioles*, and still smaller ones known as *capillaries*; capillaries merge into the smaller **VEINS,** called *venules*, and then into the larger veins, the *cavae*.

The arteries are strong, flexible hollow tubes that carry oxygenated blood from the heart to all the body's cells. Because they have to withstand greater pressure than the veins do, the arteries are more elastic, and generally larger in diameter than the veins. The arterial wall is a complex, highly structured organ made up of three layers[1]:

- The *tunica intima*, which consists of a smooth inner lining of endothelial cells in direct contact with the circulating blood, buttressed by a layer of collagen.

- The *tunica media*, a layer of muscle and elastic fibers that allows for distension as blood is pumped from the heart.

- The *tunica adventitia*, a protective layer of tough, fibrous tissue (the arterial coat).

Oxygenated blood travels via the aorta to other major arteries—such as the two femoral arteries that supply blood to the lower extremities—then into smaller arteries and arterioles, and finally into the tiny, thin-walled capillaries where the exchange of oxygen for carbon dioxide takes place. The deoxygenated blood

---

1. There are four layers if you count the collagen layer that is part of the *intima*.

enters the venules from the capillaries, then travels back to the heart via the veins. The walls of the veins have the same three coats as the arteries, but the veins are thinner and less involved in mediating blood pressure through selective constriction (vascular resistance). At intervals along some of the veins are valves that keep the blood flowing in one direction, and much of the pressure to move the blood along comes from the action of surrounding muscle that presses against the veins' walls.

The Coronary Arteries

The coronary arteries begin near the base of the aorta and, together with their many smaller branches, encircle the heart. There are two principal arteries, the right and left coronary arteries. The left artery branches off quickly to become the circumflex artery and the left anterior descending artery, and one can think of there really being *three* major coronary arteries. In most people, the main arteries are found in the same place, but there is a great deal of variation in the size and location of the many smaller branching arteries. Usually all three main arteries provide blood to the left ventricle (since it has the tough job of sending blood coursing throughout the entire body); but for ten to twenty percent of all people the right coronary artery supplies no blood to the left ventricle, and its job is taken over by branches from the other two arteries.

The left anterior descending artery provides the crucial supply of blood to the front muscles of the left ventricle, as well as to the wall that separates the left and right ventricles. The left circumflex artery travels along the outer edge of the left side of the heart, and its branches supply the side walls of the heart. The right coronary artery supplies blood to the right side of the heart, the bottom of the heart, and to the sinoatrial and, usually, atrioventricular nodes (the heart's pacemakers). The right coronary artery usually supplies the back wall of the heart via a branch called the posterior descending artery, which is present in about eighty percent of people. In the remaining twenty percent, this supply is taken over by branches from the circumflex artery.

Clearly, blockages in different coronary arteries or sections of arteries affect different sections of the heart. Since the location of branches varies from person to person, the area affected by a given blockage will similarly vary. One other factor determines the effect a particular blockage will have: the extent that a person's arterioles are capable of taking over the blood supply of the main arteries. (These arterioles are generally referred to as "collaterals.") In about eighty percent of all people, collateral vessels are able to supplement the areas that have their normal supply from the main arteries reduced by atherosclerosis. This is another reason why two people with identical blockages (in terms of location) may have very different heart disease and symptoms.

Atherosclerosis: Clogging the Arteries

Atherosclerosis is the name given to a disorder that affects the function of the arteries by thickening and obstructing their inner walls. The first signs of atherosclerosis are "fatty streaks" along the arterial wall. These fatty streaks can appear at a surprisingly early age; in fact, they have been found to be present in about eighty percent of all American teenagers. However, the disease usually progresses slowly before reaching a stage where it interferes with arterial function, and symptoms rarely become manifest before the fourth or fifth decade of life.

The impairment of function in the atherosclerotic artery is the result of plaque—or *atheromas*—along the walls of the artery, which reduce the size of the passageway blood travels through. Scientists have been working on understanding the complex process and different variables implicated in the formation of atheromas in order to find new medications to attack them at their different stages.

The smooth inner lining of the arteries is designed to keep blood moving freely and is resistant to infiltration by the diverse substances present in the blood. Resistant, but not impervious! As mentioned in the previous chapter, certain fat-bearing proteins are capable of adhering to the inner lining, where they can loosen endothelial cells and expose the collagen beneath. Platelets, minute circular cells that play an important role in the formation of blood clots, then flock to the injured site and adhere to it. The platelets (or *thrombocytes*) also release hormonelike substances called prostaglandins, which have a variety of effects on the arterial wall. Some prostaglandins cause the arteries to constrict (sometimes causing dangerous spasms); others cause them to relax; and still others cause the smooth muscle cells of the artery walls' middle layer to proliferate and extend into the inner layer. One such substance, platelet-derived growth factor, is currently the subject of intense scientific interest, and research in this area may yield valuable new information.

The net result of this cycle of injury and response is

a growing obstruction along the artery's inner wall, which becomes an easy site for yet more cholesterol-bearing LDLs to attach themselves to. These obstructions are known as atherosclerotic lesions (*lesion,* from the Latin for "a hurting," refers to any pathological change in body tissue).

The growing lesions also cause *necrosis* (death) of the inner-wall cells, which then leak their contents into the surrounding connective tissue, resulting in further tissue changes. The body's own defenses against injured or dead cells can cause still further problems when a combination of collagenous and elastic tissue forms a thick protective capsule (known as *fibrous plaque*) over the injured area. The fibrous plaque calcifies with age and reduces the elasticity of the artery, as well as obstructing blood flow. This is often accompanied by thinning of the muscular middle layer of the arterial wall, resulting in an increased likelihood of aneurysms.

An additional danger of both fatty and fibrous lesions is that they can become dislodged, causing obstructions or damage farther along the bloodstream as well as leaving behind ulcerated areas. Blood clots (thrombi) often form at the site of ulceration, and these can in turn be dislodged into the bloodstream.

All of these events take place over a considerable period of time and usually, but not necessarily, begin in the teenage years and tend to accompany each other. The course of the damage is generally as follows: 1) injury to the arterial wall; 2) proliferation of smooth muscle cells; 3) degeneration and death of cells with accompanying connective tissue changes and presence of fatty streaks; 4) repair, with accompanying thickening and calcification; and 5) appearance of "complicated lesions," continuously undergoing the aforementioned processes, along with ulceration, blood clots, and plaque debris that dislodges into the bloodstream.

CHAPTER 3

The Bypass Operation: How It Developed and What It Is

We tend to think of coronary artery disease as a uniquely twentieth-century malady, the result of a fast-paced way of life and rich, fatty foods. It is likely, however, that this ailment has been around as long as men have walked the earth. Modern scientists have used today's technology to look back into the health history of the past by examining the preserved hearts and arteries of four-thousand-year-old Egyptian mummies. Like us, the ancient Egyptians apparently suffered from a range of heart and vascular disease, including clogged arteries. The earliest written records provide further confirmation. Descriptions of symptoms that today would be identified as angina are found in the Bible and in ancient Greek texts. The second-century Greek physician Galen of Pergamum identified three different types of heart lesions, which he called *dyscrasias*, one of which may have been coronary artery disease.

Although the characteristic symptoms were noted a long time ago, the realization that a fatty diet clogged the arteries and affected the heart did not come about until many hundreds of years later. The heart was long considered the seat of emotions, the repository of the human soul, and not an organ that would suffer from disorders caused by something as mundane as diet. Lack of diagnostic tools and a long-standing taboo against dissection of human corpses delayed an understanding of the heart's actual physiology and pathology.

A few pioneers came close in the intervening years. Leonardo da Vinci was centuries ahead of his time when he drew occluded arteries in his notebooks, but this work was lost to public view until recently. It wasn't until the seventeenth century that physicians grasped the nature of blood circulation, with the first detailed description published by Dr. William Harvey in 1628. Although he identified a "third circulation" (that of the heart and arteries—systemic and pulmonary circulation were known before), no connection was made between it and death from heart disease. Eighteenth-century British physicians—notably William Heberden—came to recognize the characteristics of angina and regard it as a serious disorder, and Dr. Edward Jenner noted the association of angina pains with arterial degeneration.

The modern understanding of heart disease was first articulated by Dr. James Herrick in a paper published in 1912. Dr. Herrick's work was a careful synthesis of the body of knowledge then available; he not only gave a detailed description of the disease but catalogued many of the personality types and life-styles we have come to associate with it. Still, it took a surprisingly long time for his ideas to become widespread in the medical community.

In the twentieth century, a better comprehension of the nature and causes of heart disease came hand in hand with improved technology that allowed more precise diagnoses. The scientific advances ushered in the modern era of open-heart surgery. Valve replacements, artificial pacemakers, transplanted hearts, and the coronary bypass operation have given many heart patients an extra lease on life.

The coronary bypass operation has come such a long way since its debut that it is easy to forget the procedure has been part of our medical arsenal for less than twenty-five years. Two remarkable inventions are largely responsible for making the operation, and its subsequent refinements, possible. The first is the coronary arteriogram or angiogram, which is a form of cardiac catheterization. The second is the heart-lung machine, which allows blood to continue circulating after the heart has been stilled.

The story of the first cardiac catheterization is a remarkable one in the annals of medicine. Werner Forssman, a young German doctor, believed that a catheter could be safely and easily inserted into the living, beating human heart. This would help to solve the problem of how to take finely detailed pictures of an organ that is completely composed of soft tissue, which does not show up well on X-rays. Forssman used the technique successfully on animals, but was refused permission to try it with human volunteers. In 1929 he passed a catheter through a vein in *his own* arm and threaded it up to his heart. He then walked up the stairs to the radiology lab and ordered the horrified attendant to take X-rays, thus proving that the heart could safely be catheterized. (Other versions of the story have Forssman calmly dictating notes while he catheterized himself.)

Dr. Forssman lost his job at the time, but his achievement proved a boon to the medical world and he was awarded the Nobel Prize in later life. Dr. Forssman's heroic act of altruistic experimentation led to the next major step in diagnosing heart disease almost thirty years later: injecting a nontoxic dye directly into the heart to make the pumping ventricles visible on an X-ray screen. Around the same time, in 1959, Dr. Mason Sones, Jr., of the Cleveland Clinic passed a catheter into a coronary artery and realized that it was possible to visualize the insides of the arteries themselves and determine the extent of any blockage or narrowing. Today, cardiac catheters are used to picture the heart's chambers and the arteries, to take blood-pressure readings at their source, and to take blood samples from the heart's own supply. Doctors are thus able to predict and forestall potentially fatal disturbances of the heart's blood supply.

The other giant technological step was the heart-lung machine, designed to get around the central problem of how to operate on a heart that was still beating. Doctors had learned that the heart could be stopped and restarted, but without a circulating blood supply irreparable brain and other organ system damage would occur within three minutes. The first models of a machine that could take over blood circulation from the heart were developed by Dr. John H. Gibbon of Philadelphia. He worked on his invention for twenty-two years before it was ready to be successfully used on a human being in 1953.

In order for a machine successfully to take over the heart's function, even for just a few hours, three main obstacles need to be overcome. The first is replacing the lungs' job of resupplying the oxygen taken up by the body's cells. The second is keeping the blood circulating at sufficient pressure to penetrate every cell in the body, but not to pump it at such force that there are any injuries to the proteins and vital red and white cells carried in the blood, or to the blood vessels or the body's cells. The third obstacle is to keep the heart stationary and healthy while it is being operated on.

Supplying oxygen to the blood seems a relatively simple matter: why not bubble oxygen through it as you do water in a fish tank? This is exactly what the first heart-lung machines did, but then a new difficulty emerged. Not all the oxygen is absorbed by the red blood cells, and, particularly in the early stages of development, there was a risk of air bubbles traveling inside the bloodstream and causing embolisms. Various filters were used to keep out extra air bubbles, including a system of whirling disks to spin the oxygen through the blood.

Early attempts to solve the above problems were not particularly successful. The heart-lung machines of twenty or thirty years ago were able to take over the blood circulation and sustain life for short periods of time, but the risk of mortality and complications with these early machines was extremely high. So high, in fact, that many physicians did not believe that a truly efficient heart-lung machine was possible. For a short time, human volunteers even acted as the perfusion equipment to take over the blood supply of the patient—a procedure that potentially ran the risk of a two-hundred-percent mortality rate.

Today's oxygenators get around the problem by imitating the way the lungs' own cell membranes work. In these machines, blood and oxygen are separated from each other by a very fine artificial membrane and the oxygen is absorbed into the blood through osmosis. Advances in the pumping machinery allow the pumps to be fine-tuned during the operation and to circulate the blood efficiently but more gently. These pumps come much closer to paralleling the lungs' activity and the heart's wavelike contractions, but still do not quite equal the efficiency of the real thing. For this reason, surgeons seek to keep to a minimum the period that the heart is "on total bypass." (This is the term used to describe taking over the heart's functions by machine. It should not be confused with "bypass surgery," which refers to the use of other blood vessels to bypass blocked sections of the coronary arteries.)

Drug therapy during the operation has further helped to minimize trauma from the heart-lung machine. Blood cells react badly when they contact the metal and plastic parts of the machine, and there is a tendency for clots to form. To obviate this, heparin (an anticlotting drug) is administered to the patient. When the operation is over, protamine (a drug derived from fish) is given to restore the blood's clotting ability.

The critical moment in using the heart-lung machine comes when the heart is stopped. The early method of stilling the heart was to use a combination of cold (mild hypothermia), anoxic arrest (cutting off the supply of oxygen by clamping the aorta shut), and ventricular fibrillation. The importance of cooling the heart to reduce its need for oxygen was noted early on, and this led to the development of a means of stilling the heart by cooling it very rapidly. In 1976, a technique called cold potassium cardioplegia was introduced to stop the heart, and its use soon became widespread. The advantage of cold potassium mixed with dilute blood is that it instantly stops the heart and does not let it slowly wind down to a halt, since the extra beats might use up valuable nutrients and oxygen.

What Is the Bypass Operation?

In the previous chapter we described how the coronary arteries provide the heart's own blood supply and how their function can become impaired by atherosclerosis. The ideal cure would be if we could somehow remove all traces of plaque in the artery, reduce the thickening of the intimal layer, and restore the arterial muscles' elasticity. Since this is not possible (except in an extremely limited way, as described in the chapter on alternative treatments), doctors do the next best thing: graft a healthy, unoccluded blood vessel to bypass the blocked areas of the coronary arteries.

The usual blood vessel for the graft is the saphenous vein. We have several of these veins in each leg; they are the same ones that are affected by varicose veins. The saphenous vein is removed from the leg much the way it would be in a varicose-vein operation, and while patients may feel some pain from the incisions, the vein removal generally causes no serious impairment to the leg's blood supply. To remove the necessary vein, an incision about half an inch deep has to be made in the leg along the length of the vein to be used. The vein is then carefully removed and the skin is stitched back together. The vein is meticulously examined to make sure that it is usable and that there are no leaks anywhere along it. People with cardiovascular disease do not always have the healthiest blood vessels, and sometimes several incisions have to be made before locating a workable vein.

The vein will be cut into several appropriately sized sections, depending on the number of bypasses. One end of the vein will be sewn into a small incision in the aorta, the body's largest artery, which is located just above the heart. Since veins have one-way valves inside them to keep the blood moving back to the heart, the vein will be upside down, in the reverse position from its location in the leg. The other end of the vein will be attached to the coronary artery, just beyond the site of the occlusion. This is the most delicate and important part of the operation, since the vein is about the diameter of a drinking straw and the coronary artery is a mere fraction of that width (from 1 to 1.5 millimeters, or about the diameter of pencil lead).

The grafting process takes place with the heart stopped and the blood supply taken over by the heart-lung machine. Several vein grafts (and possibly a graft using the internal mammary artery—a blood vessel in the inner chest wall) will be performed, depending on the number of blockages in the coronary arteries. When the surgeon is satisfied that all the new conduits are firmly attached and viable, he or she will restart the heart and take the patient off the heart-lung machine. The bypassed blood vessels will immediately provide the heart with an improved blood supply.

This improvement will be maintained for as long as the new conduits do not become clogged by atherosclerosis or blood clots. With vein grafts, good flow generally lasts at least five to ten years, with some deterioration after that as the veins begin to clog up again. After the operation, it is really in the patient's hands to make sure that the risk factors for atherosclerosis are greatly reduced. With better postoperative life-style management and medication, the bypass patient can expect a greater-than-fifty-percent opening in the grafted veins for as long as twelve years and possibly even longer.

Variations on a Theme

Sometimes, on the beach or around the swimming pool, informal gatherings of middle-aged and older men will form to show off their chest scars and boast the number of bypass grafts their surgeon has performed on them. Interestingly enough, while the man with the quintuple bypass may win the beach "zipper club" competition, the correlation between the number of bypass grafts received and the severity of illness overcome is not a strict ratio. Surgeons today are inclined to use more grafts—or, in doctors' parlance, "revascularize more thoroughly"—to make sure there is an adequate blood supply should any single graft fail to remain open. Most bypasses today are at least "triple," meaning three new conduits of arterial blood were created. Although they may seem more alarming or impressive, quadruple, or even quintuple, bypasses are no longer particularly unusual.

The other major variation, besides the number of grafts, is whether or not the doctor chooses to use one or both internal mammary arteries (also known as the internal thoracic arteries) instead of a vein. About seventy percent of all bypass operations now involve the use of the internal mammary artery, although this figure may be much higher in some centers than in others. While using the internal mammary artery graft is technically more difficult—and may require a longer operation, a reason some doctors don't like to use the technique—the growing evidence is that such grafts are more efficient and stay open longer.

There are several natural advantages to using the internal mammary arteries, which carry blood to a small section of the chest wall, to resupply the coronary arteries. One is that they have their own blood supply—unlike the saphenous veins, which have to be grafted onto the aorta as well as to the coronary artery they are bypassing. Only one end of the internal mammary artery has to be detached, and interruptions to the blood supply are consequently less likely.

Another plus is that they are more elastic than veins, have stronger walls, and are more effectively self-regulated because of their greater production of prostacyclin, a chemical that controls the artery muscles. Although the size of the opening—or lumen—is smaller than that of the saphenous veins, the internal thoracic artery is more responsive to changes in blood-flow demand, dilating or contracting according to need. The thicker, more elastic arterial walls may be better able to withstand fluctuations in blood pressure.

For these reasons, and perhaps because of other factors that are as yet unknown, the internal mammary artery grafts stay open longer (have a better *patency rate*) than vein grafts—approximately ninety percent after twelve years, versus less than fifty percent. This means that they are less liable to become clogged by blood clots or atherosclerosis—both during the crucial period immediately following the operation, and over the ensuing years. A paper recently presented to the American Heart Association pointed out that there is a higher ten-year survival rate when the internal mammary artery is used to revascularize the left anterior descending artery than when saphenous vein grafts are used alone. In addition, heart attacks, reoperation, and the need for hospitalization for other cardiac events also decrease under selected circumstances.

As the evidence for increased long-term survival for patients who have internal mammary artery grafts continues to grow, this variation on the procedure is becoming more and more a standard part of the operation. It is also increasingly being used in cases where it was once thought too difficult or where briefer operations were considered optimal: notably for women and the elderly. Variations using bilateral internal mammary arteries or using free grafts of these arteries (i.e., removing both sides of the artery and reattaching in the same way as would be done with the saphenous veins) are also becoming more frequently performed, although still controversial.

The history of coronary artery bypass surgery is ongoing, and every year sees new innovations in the technique and in the technology. The mortality rate has been going down, better results than ever before are being achieved with older patients and with patients with poor ventricular function, and the blood vessels used for bypass are remaining unclogged for longer periods. For now, bypass is the best solution for many people suffering from coronary artery disease. In a few years, other less invasive or more effective solutions may be available . . . although these are not quite imminent enough to make it worth putting off the operation in the hope that something better will come along.

CHAPTER 4

How Do I Know If I Need Bypass Surgery? Symptoms and Medical Tests

John, a fifty-four-year-old construction foreman, had been suffering from chest pains for the past four years. If he forgot himself and hurried on the construction site or so much as threw a few baskets with his teenage son, he would get breathless and develop a crushing feeling in his chest. The discomfort would subside soon after he stopped to rest and placed a nitroglycerin tablet under his tongue. These attacks occurred only once or twice a week (as is typical of the condition referred to as stable angina), and his cardiologist felt he could do well with medical therapy, especially as John was diligent in taking his medications.

John began to get anxious that at his young age he was dependent on so many different types of pills. Both his father and uncle had suffered heart attacks, and John found himself always worrying that physical exer-

tion might lead to an episode of angina . . . which might not be relieved by nitroglycerin. His relationship with friends, and indeed with his wife and children, began to suffer as he focused more on anticipation of his chest pain and less on the world around him. When his angina stepped up to once or twice a day, John consulted his cardiologist, confiding his fears. An angiogram revealed severe narrowing in John's coronary arteries, and subsequent bypass surgery relieved him of his bouts of chest pain and of the strain in his relationships.

Angina is actually not so much a disease in itself as a *symptom* of transient cardiac ischemia, a temporary interruption in the blood flow through the coronary arteries. The cells of the heart muscle use oxygen very efficiently, but they will starve and die from lack of oxygen (ischemia) in as short a period as twenty minutes. Temporary or partial interruptions in coronary blood flow cause the painful, squeezing sensation referred to as angina. This can occur for a number of reasons.

The most common reason for people with narrowed arteries to suffer an ischemic attack is an increase in the workload of the heart muscle during physical activity. Exertion of any kind requires the heart to pump harder and faster, activity that needs to be fueled by a larger quantity of blood than the narrowed arteries are able to provide. Since stopping that activity—whether it's walking, climbing stairs, or running—decreases the demand for extra oxygen, many angina sufferers find that upon stopping to rest the pain abates on its own. Stress, digesting a heavy meal, or exposure to cold, also can trigger episodes of angina.

A nitroglycerin tablet placed under the tongue will also make the pain disappear as if by magic. The "nitro" causes blood vessels to dilate, or open up, thus increasing the supply of blood from the coronary arteries as well as reducing the amount of work the heart has to do to circulate blood throughout the rest of the body. Nitroglycerin should work in three to five minutes. If your chest pain continues after you have taken the pills and/or lasts longer than five minutes after you stop exercising, you should repeat the dosage. If this does not stop the pain, seek emergency medical treatment immediately, as you could be having a heart attack.

Another reason the nitroglycerin may not work is if you have had the pills around for too long or have been storing them outside of their glass containers. The medicine loses its potency quickly, especially if exposed to heat, moisture, or light. You should be sure to replace the pills whenever they are nearing the expiration date printed on the bottle they came in, and you should always keep an extra supply on hand.

Exertion is not the only source of angina attacks. Blood clots or plaque debris dislodged from an atheroma can temporarily block an artery and cause angina pain. If the clot does not get broken up or dissolve, the ischemic attack can turn from a temporary bout into a full-fledged heart attack.

Another cause of transient ischemic attacks is Prinzmetal's angina (named after the doctor who first described it). In this condition, sudden spasms can cause the coronary arteries to close off. The immediate reason for these spasms is not known, although they usually occur close to the site of atheromas and are rare in people who do not have arteriosclerosis. Prinzmetal's angina is also known as variant angina. Not being mediated by physical activity, it can occur without warning and at any time. In some people, the attacks often occur at the same time each day, but it is not yet known why this should be the case.

The transient bouts of ischemia that produce angina do not necessarily destroy cardiac muscle. If the ischemia lasts for a while, however, the cells of the heart's muscles may begin to die—a condition known as infarction, or a "heart attack." The severity of the attack depends on whether the blockage is total, how long it lasts, and whether the heart's electrical system is also affected. If the heart attack prevents the left ventricle from circulating blood, death will occur within a few minutes as a consequence of the interruption to the brain's supply of oxygen.

Both transitory and deadly ischemic attacks can also occur without any apparent symptoms. In *Heart Talk*—Peter and Joan Cohn's excellent book on "silent" ischemia—the well-known Italian cardiologist Attilio Maseri describes how he first realized that patients could have asymptomatic coronary artery blockages.

> I remember seeing an abnormality that I usually associated with pain on the electrocardiographic monitor at the nurse's station outside the patient's room. I rushed inside to find him calmly reading a book. "Do you have pain?" I asked. "Who me?" he said, very obviously surprised. "No, no pain." I went back to the monitor and the huge injury wave was still there. A nitroglycerin under the tongue made it go away just as it would if he had pain. That convinced me he had ischemia. . . .

Silent ischemia affects at least five percent of all adult Americans, resulting in fifty thousand deaths a year from heart attacks that arise without any prior warning. Silent ischemia also affects most—and possibly all—angina sufferers. In other words, a person with angina may have several attacks every day that he does not know about!

The news is not all bad, since several of the tests we will be describing are capable of alerting your physician to the possibility that you could have asymptomatic ischemia. The difficulty for the patient is that the checks and balances that would ordinarily prompt an adjustment of medication or a trip to the doctor may be completely absent or capricious. In other words, if you experience crushing chest pain every time you bicycle for more than five minutes, you will remember to take your medication and you will probably give serious thought to having bypass surgery. If you experience no pain, you are more likely to continue exercising to the point of doing real damage to your heart, and you are likely to be psychologically less willing to undergo surgery.

Mary Catherine, a seventy-year-old retired librarian, had been having anginal chest pains for the past fifteen years. Multiple electrocardiograms done in her doctor's office showed her condition to be stable, and she was maintained on a somewhat increasing but effective medical regimen. Mary Catherine became worried when the frequency of her pains increased to three or four times a day, sometimes occurring without stress or physical exertion. One morning she had two hours of continuous chest pain which was only partially relieved by seven nitroglycerin tablets. She called her doctor, who instructed her to meet him at the emergency room of the local hospital for admission for coronary angiography and possible surgery.

While you should not spend all your time worrying about your heart condition, you should be sure to contact your doctor if your pattern of angina changes in duration or severity. Angina is considered *stable* if the pattern of chest pain is regular over the course of at least six months, and if the source of the attacks—for example, exertion, emotional stress—is reasonably evident. *Unstable* angina is recognizable by a change in the normal pattern, with chest pain occurring with unusual frequency or for no discernible reason. Unstable angina may be a predictor of an impending heart attack, and it should always be monitored closely.

The following tests are used to check whether you have coronary artery disease and how far it has progressed, as well as to help determine the success of a particular course of treatment.

Chest X-Ray

After the physical examination, the most common general test your family physician or cardiologist will conduct to determine the health of your heart is the chest X-ray. The X-rays are usually taken from the back and from the side, with the patient remaining stationary so the different angles can be compared. The chest X-ray does not provide detailed information about the coronary arteries, but it can supply important clues to the presence of heart disease and to the state of the lungs as well. The heart appears as a shadow on the X-ray film; the size and shape of the shadow can indicate the presence of abnormalities. If the lungs are filled with fluid, this can be a sign of congestive heart failure (insufficient pressure or insufficient blood being pumped from the left ventricle). X-rays are painless and the whole process takes no more than a few minutes. Since a small amount of radiation is passed through your body for each X-ray, it is a good idea to keep track of your X-rays and to have them on hand when you consult any new physician.

The Electrocardiogram (ECG)

The ECG provides a record of the heart's electrical activity. Since a heartbeat is created by a standard pattern of electrical charges, the ECG can not only determine whether something is wrong, but which part of the heart is affected. There are three forms of electrocardiogram: the "resting" or baseline ECG, the "stress test," and the ambulatory ECG (also known as Holter monitoring).

To take an ECG reading, the doctor begins by attaching six to twelve "leads" at various points on the patient's chest and limbs. The doctor may move these leads around to provide different "views" of the heart's activity. The leads are attached with a light adhesive and are easily removable. They convey the electrical impulses of the heart to a monitor and do not have any electrical charge of their own, so they cannot give you a shock or stimulate you in any way.

For the resting ECG, a reading is taken while the patient is standing or sitting at ease. The process takes only a few moments. It is a poor indicator of coronary artery disease, however, as many people with moderate to severely narrowed arteries do not show any abnormalities in the ECG while at rest. For the stress ECG, the patient is asked to perform progressively more strenuous activity—such as walking on a treadmill or climbing up and down a set of steps. This test indicates how the heart responds to an increased demand for oxygen. It is a better indicator of coronary artery disease than the resting ECG, with over ninety percent accuracy for patients suffering from triple-vessel disease . . . but it is less reliable for people who have only a single or two arteries affected.

Both the resting and the stress ECG are extremely safe procedures, although a very, very small number of patients have had heart attacks during the stress test. The likelihood of this happening is extremely slight, and you are at considerably less risk exerting yourself in the doctor's office than you might be walking upstairs or hurrying to catch a bus on your own. Your doctor will be closely watching how the exercise is affecting your heart and will stop the test if you show any signs of putting undue pressure on your heart muscle. If you feel any discomfort or nausea during the test, be sure to alert the nurse or doctor immediately.

Since the presence of ischemia is inconstant and unpredictable—depending on factors affecting the interior lumen (opening) of the arteries that are still poorly understood—it may be absent during exercise and yet still occur at other times during the day. For this reason, your physician may ask you to wear a Holter monitor, or ambulatory ECG, which provides a record of every heartbeat over a twenty-four to forty-eight-hour period. It enables the doctor to detect ischemic attacks that might otherwise go unnoticed, indicating how often and under what circumstances such attacks might occur.

Before providing you with the Holter monitor, the

doctor will first attach electrodes to your chest, as for any ECG—but these particular leads connect to a small recording device about the size of a Walkman cassette player. You will be asked to wear the electrodes and carry the monitoring device throughout the day and while you sleep. You will also be asked to record any symptoms of angina as they occur during the day, as well as to make note of the time of such events as mealtimes, exercise, stressful situations (such as driving an automobile in traffic), and when you use the bathroom. The ECG results can then be correlated with these events, and the reason for any abnormalities better diagnosed. The results of the ECG are usually fed through a computer that is able to read them at high speed and alert the doctor to any unusual signs. The newest models of Holter monitor come with their own microchip computers, allowing them to provide feedback to the patients wearing them.

The ECG provides a permanent record of the heart's electrical activity, appearing on graph paper in the form of a continuous line with waves, dips, and rises. These fluctuations in the line are assigned a letter of the alphabet to describe them. An important indication for the presence of coronary artery disease is an abnormality of the ST segment. The "depressed" ST segment is considered to be a reliable sign of coronary atherosclerosis. The point of onset, the duration of ST segment abnormalities, and the point at which they disappear during the stress test provide useful information regarding the extent of the disease. Should your ECGs show depressed ST segments, your doctor will usually call for one or all of the following tests.

Radioisotope Scans

There are three main types of radioisotope scans: 1) thallium-201, 2) technetium pyrophosphate, and 3) multiple-gated blood pool scans.

In all three scans, a small amount of radioactive material is injected into the bloodstream via a vein. As the blood circulates through the heart, the progress of the radioactive particles is monitored by a special camera that records gamma radiation.

The thallium test is the one used to confirm a diagnosis of coronary artery disease and is the most accurate noninvasive test to analyze this disease. Thallium isotopes are able to pass from the bloodstream into the cell walls of the heart. The gamma cameras record this absorption, and the parts of the heart that are being starved of arterial blood show up as "cold spots" where the thallium was not absorbed. Thallium tests are usually conducted in the hospital on an outpatient basis. The most reliable results are obtained if the patient is given a thallium scan during the peak activity period in a stress test, followed by additional scans after the patient has rested for two hours.

Technetium pyrophosphate is a radioisotope that binds to a substance that seeks out injured tissue. Injured areas of the heart show up on the gamma camera as "hot spots." Technetium pyrophosphate is usually used to determine whether the patient has sustained a heart attack and how much damage to the heart has occurred. Since impairment of the left ventricle's function is an important consideration in determining whether bypass surgery is warranted, this test is often called for to see how much damage the left ventricle has sustained.

Blood pool scanning—which is also known as multiple-gated angiography (MUGA) or radionuclide cine angiogram (RNCA)—provides a portrait of heartbeats in action. A small amount of the patient's own blood is removed and the red blood cells are marked with a radioactive tracer. The blood is then reinjected into a vein to mix with the body's blood pool. (Remember, the entire blood pool passes through the heart about every sixty seconds.) The gamma camera is hooked up to a computer, which synchronizes it to create a series of "gated" pictures of the heart's cycle of contraction and relaxation. The physician is thus able to get a moving picture of the heart's function.

The Echocardiogram

Pictures taken using high-frequency sound waves (ultrasound) are another way the physician can examine the heart at work. The echocardiogram cannot provide a visualization of the coronary arteries, but it can demonstrate impaired function, valve damage, and increased thickness of the ventricular walls. The echocardiogram thus provides useful information on functional damage wrought by ischemia, as well as helping to distinguish other possible causes behind the patient's chest pain (such as mitrovalve prolapse or hypertrophic cardiomyopathy) whose symptoms may closely mimic coronary artery disease.

Doppler ultrasonography is another form of ultrasound testing that your physician may employ. It is not used to examine the coronary arteries directly, but rather to provide detailed information about the blood flow of major arteries and veins elsewhere in your body. Doppler ultrasonography is painless and completely harmless. For this test, a transducer—an instrument which emits and receives sound waves—is passed along the skin over the area to be examined. The Doppler can detect sections of a blood vessel where the flow is reduced, and is useful to diagnose aortic stenosis, venous insufficiency, and arterial occlusion or trauma. It can also be used to diagnose valve and cardiac muscle disorders.

Other Noninvasive Tests

Magnetic resonance imaging (MRI), computerized tomography (CT) scans, and positron emission tomography (PET) scans are highly sophisticated techniques for examining soft tissue. While these techniques can be used for diagnosing coronary artery disease, they are considerably more expensive than angiography, which yields comparable results, and are therefore rarely employed for this purpose unless other questions exist.

The Coronary Angiogram

The most efficient and accurate test for coronary artery disease is also the one doctors usually recommend last and about which patients may have the most fears. The coronary angiogram is considered an "invasive" procedure, because a thin, flexible catheter is inserted into an artery or vein and threaded through the blood vessel until it enters the heart itself.

Patients are often anxious about submitting to angiography—and may put off having it done—because the procedure is invasive, is performed while the patient is awake and aware of what is going on, and because it is generally the deciding diagnostic test as to whether bypass surgery is needed. There are risks in coronary angiography, but many people are more afraid of the *results* than of the test itself. Coronary artery disease is something where what you don't know *can* hurt you, and you should not let your fears make your decisions for you.

The tremendous value of the angiogram as a diagnostic and preventive tool greatly outweighs its disadvantages. Indeed, for about ninety-nine percent of patients, angiography is completely safe, virtually painless (since there are few nerve endings in the arteries), and more boring than unpleasant. In major hospitals that frequently apply the procedure—and provided that the angiogram is not being done in an emergency, such as a heart attack—the mortality rate is considerably less than one percent.

The risk of the procedure comes from the possibility of it dislodging or loosening a portion of the plaque on the arterial wall. Such a dislodged piece is known as an *embolus* or *embolism*. The embolus can travel through the bloodstream and cause a deadly blockage in the brain or in the heart. A similar problem occurs if the catheter dislodges a blood clot (*thrombus*). More effective "clot-busting" drugs have recently come on the market, and these have greatly enhanced the safety of coronary catheterization.

Another risk associated with cardiac catheterization is that the heart's electrical system might somehow be temporarily disturbed. If the pacemakers that control the sequence of electrical charges start to "fire" out of order, the heart flutters or fibrillates instead of beating.

Ventricular fibrillation is the most deadly electrical disturbance; since no blood is being circulated, death or irreversible brain damage can occur within three minutes. It is almost always possible to restart the electrical sequence and throw it back on track by applying an electrical charge to the heart. This has to be done immediately, and it is not always successful. It should be noted that the likelihood of ventricular fibrillation occurring during a coronary angiogram is not great, and that it is unlikely to take place in a patient who does not already have problems with electrical conductivity or damaged sinoatrial nodes.

Having mentioned the risk attached to the coronary angiogram, it is worth noting that the procedure *saves* many lives every year. For those people who are referred for the test, their greatest risk is of a fatal heart attack if the coronary artery condition is not diagnosed and treated effectively.

Before you go in for a coronary angiogram, your physician—who will have already discussed its necessity with a group of specialists—will explain the risks to you and ask you to sign a consent form. Do not be alarmed by the legalistic language of the consent form, which presents a "worst-case" scenario. It is merely a formality. Also, your doctor may give you specific directions to follow before going for the angiogram—such as not eating for a certain number of hours prior to the examination.

Before the test begins, you will usually be given a mild tranquilizer—such as Valium—to keep you relaxed during the procedure. Be sure to tell the doctor whether you are currently taking other tranquilizers or medication, and if you have ever had a bad reaction to a particular tranquilizer (a small percentage of people find that certain tranquilizers make them anxious or disoriented).

Next, you will be asked to lie on a special table that can be maneuvered into different positions. Before inserting the catheters, the medical staff will shave any hair at the site and clean the skin with an antibacterial solution. You will then be given a local anesthetic at the places where the catheters are to be inserted. You will *not* be put to sleep, and your doctors may offer to let you watch the interior of your own heart on the X-ray screen.

Two catheters are usually used: one in the femoral artery near the groin, and one in the femoral vein, also in the groin area. Under some circumstances, the arm veins may be used. The catheters are threaded up to the heart, with the entire procedure taking place under X-ray fluoroscopy. Once the catheters are in place, they can be used to provide a variety of different readings—including the heart's blood pressure and gas plasma levels—as well as to inject the contrast medium.

The material that makes it possible to visualize the coronary arteries is a radiographic contrast dye. When the dye is injected, you will probably feel a very warm sensation deep in your chest that lasts for about a minute then fades completely away. The contrast medium is injected several times to provide different views of the heart, and each time it is used you will feel this warm flash. (Usually your physician will tell you just before the dye is injected, or you can ask him or her to do so.) The dye may be injected into the chambers of the heart, particularly the left ventricle, to allow the doctors to see how well they are functioning. It will also be injected directly into the coronary arteries, where obstructions will be revealed as negative areas that the dye does not flow through.

After you have been turned and manipulated in all kinds of positions to provide all different angles for the X-rays, the catheters will be removed. The total catheterization procedure usually takes twenty minutes to an hour, depending on the number of viewpoints the physicians feel are necessary. It's not over yet, however, but the worst certainly is. To prevent bleeding from the femoral artery, a nurse or physician will apply manual pressure to the site of catheter insertion for some twenty minutes or so. You will then be asked to lie for the next six hours with a heavy sandbag on the incision area to prevent any possible oozing. You will also be asked to drink some fluids, since the contrast medium is a diuretic. This is not the easiest thing in the world when you are lying flat on your back, but you should try to comply as best you can.

Once again, it is important to remember that coronary angiography may provide vital information about the health of your coronary arteries. There is very little to fear from the procedure, except for a few hours of tedium.

Interpreting and Understanding the Results

As we have seen, every case of cardiovascular disease is different. The factors that affect the diagnosis include which arteries in particular and how many of them are affected, the extent of arterial *stenosis* (narrowing), the extent of damage already suffered by the heart muscle, the age of the patient, and his/her history of heart attacks or strokes. However, physicians agree on three test results that call unquestionably for bypass surgery if there are no major contraindications.

1. *Left Main Disease*. Stenosis of the left main branch (before it divides into the circumflex and left anterior descending arteries) is the strongest indication that bypass surgery is needed. Pa-

tients with left main branch blockages have
a greater than fifty percent mortality rate over
a five-year period, and an eighty to ninety
percent mortality rate for seven to ten years after diagnosis. If you have left main disease,
your physician will probably want to schedule
you for surgery as soon as possible to prevent any risk of a fatal or severely damaging
heart attack.

2. *Triple Vessel Disease*. Blockages of seventy percent or more in three arteries, particularly if
combined with any heart muscle damage. The extent of stenosis in the left anterior descending
artery is particularly important here, and, if severe, is often considered to require bypass surgery even if only one or no other artery is affected.
Recent findings demonstrate that patients with
triple vessel disease not only have their quality
of life considerably improved by bypass surgery, but also their longevity is greatly enhanced.

3. *Impaired Function of the Left Ventricle*. The muscles of the left ventricle can be extensively damaged by heart attacks or by prolonged bouts of
ischemia. This interferes with the crucial function of the left ventricle: to pump arterial blood
throughout the body. While bypass surgery cannot restore life to cells that have died, it can improve the ability of the remaining myocardial
cells to do their work and can prevent further,
possibly fatal, ischemic injury. The extent of
damage to left ventricular function can be measured by two things: the ejection fraction (the
percentage of blood inside the left ventricle that

is ejected with each contraction); and the end diastolic pressure, the blood pressure measured inside the left ventricle (by cardiac catheter) when it is most relaxed between beats. Coronary bypass surgery is feasible, and indeed strongly recommended, for patients with ejection fractions of twenty to forty percent.

Any or all of the above conditions usually are clear indications for bypass surgery, but other reasons should not be ruled out. You should base your decision as to whether to have the operation on the degree of coronary artery illness ascertained by the various tests, the extent to which angina interferes with your life-style, your response to medications and willingness to make medication part of your daily routine, and how aggressively you want to treat the disease. (For more in-depth discussion of alternative treatments, please refer to Chapter Eight.)

CHAPTER 5

What's Involved in the Bypass Operation?

Once you and your doctors have decided on bypass surgery, they will usually try to schedule the operation for sometime soon, usually within a few weeks. There is little point in delaying, since this may only cause you more anxiety and increases the time available for a blood clot or other obstruction to form.

There are a number of things you can do to get the best use out of this waiting period. Think of it as an opportunity to learn more about the operation. One way to do so is for both you and your family to take advantage of the patient education programs provided by most good hospitals. You will get a better idea of what to expect from your hospital stay, the things you can practice beforehand, and how your family can be supportive. The more you can take part in your own treatment, the less helpless and uncertain you will be during the pre- and postoperative period. The same holds true for members of your family, who will have their own fears to contend with at the same time as they want to be completely supportive to you.

"I was very worried beforehand about my father's operation," said Amy. "My mother and I would try to be cheerful around him, and then we'd bicker with each other . . . something we never used to do. After we watched the films and talked to the hospital staff, we felt much better. They told us exactly what they were going to be doing for Dad, and they took all our apprehensions very seriously. We still knew there was a very small risk in the procedure, but at least we knew exactly what to expect. Not knowing what was going on was the worst. Once we knew, my mother and I even stopped fighting."

The patient education program will provide you with detailed information about the operation itself. You will also be given some practical guidelines to make things easier for yourself afterward—such as instructions on driving, showering, et cetera, following the operation.

You can also practice coughing with a hard pillow clutched tightly against your chest, a process known as "splinting." After the operation, you need to cough to keep your lungs free of any liquid that can build up inside them. The chest wound can make such coughing uncomfortable unless you hold tightly on to an object that will keep the chest wall still.

An additional step you can take during the waiting period is to bank some of your own blood or have a friend or member of the family with your blood type make a donation in your name. Be sure to check with your physician before you give blood yourself. There is usually no problem for people with stable angina and good ventricular function, but it is essential you ask your doctor first. Up to two pints of blood are all you are likely to need, as bypass surgery generally does not involve much blood loss. Since the operation is planned to be elective, the surgeons do not have to open the chest in a hurry and can take the time to prevent bleeding. Also, any blood around the incision can be siphoned off and filtered through the heart-lung machine to be returned to the patient's body.

You may also wish to practice some relaxation techniques, which can be helpful in relieving anxiety and letting you stay calm during the recovery period. A common cause of patient discomfort in the postoperative period occurs when they resist the respirator, and this is a good time to put relaxation techniques in practice. The hospital education program should be able to help you here, or you can pick up some self-hypnosis/relaxation books or tapes at your local bookstore.

Unless your operation is an emergency, you will first meet your cardiothoracic surgeon some days or even weeks before the procedure is performed. This meeting is an important one, but it does not need to be stressful. The surgeon generally meets with you in his or her office, wearing street clothes rather than surgical scrubs, and should be open to any questions you may have.

The surgeon will have reviewed the results of your angiogram (which are preserved on thirty-five-millimeter film) as well as of your other tests, and will want to explain what these results mean. He or she will also tell you more about what the operation entails, which arteries will be bypassed, and what improvements in health you can expect the operation to produce. The surgeon will inform you as to which medications you will be able to do without following the operation, as well as which ones you will still need. If you wish, you will be shown the relevant parts of the film made of your angiogram. The surgeon will also tell you what the risks of the procedure are, as well as the risks of not having it performed at this time. (Occasionally, the tests will suggest to the surgeon that you should try a period of medical maintenance before having the operation.)

The meeting is a good time for you to voice your fears and concerns. Do not be afraid to ask any question that occurs to you, even if it strikes you as "silly." There are no silly questions in this business, and it is better to have a concern allayed than to let it bother you.

You will generally be scheduled to come into the hospital a full day before the surgery. This may seem a bit of a nuisance to you, but it allows the hospital to make sure all your tests and records are in order. The surgeon will want to have the most up-to-date results before operating on you, and you can expect to have an ECG, a chest X-ray, several blood tests, and urinalysis at this time. You may be interviewed by a number of different specialists, and you may find yourself answering the same questions over again to the different doctors. You will also have your blood pressure, pulse, and physical examination repeated several times. You will probably have had these tests performed a short while before, but having them done again is to your benefit. Even a low-grade infection or other health anomaly could interfere with your recovery from surgery.

The night before the operation is also when you will get to meet your anesthesiologist, who will explain his or her role to you. The anesthesiologist makes sure you are sufficiently drugged that you do not feel any pain, but not so doped up that coming off the anesthetic is a problem. The anesthesiologist also has the vital task of controlling your breathing and blood pressure during the operation. Make sure you tell the anesthesiologist about any medication you have taken recently and whether you have ever had adverse drug reactions.

By having you stay at the hospital, the doctors can also be sure that you do not eat anything for at least eight hours before the operation. The reason is that anesthesia is safer on an empty stomach. You will be given dinner in the early evening, but no additional food for the eight hours prior to the operation. You can request ice chips or some hard "sucking" candy if you are thirsty during the night, or in the morning. You will also be given a sleeping medication to make sure you are well rested before your operation. This sleeping medication will not interfere with your anesthetic on the following day.

Before the operation itself, you will be scrubbed clean, and some of your body hair will be shaved. You will also be asked to remove all jewelry, eyeglasses or contact lenses, and dentures. Some people find this process somewhat humiliating, but it is done in your own interest to reduce the risk of infection. If your operation is scheduled for the first thing in the morning, the scrubbing and shaving may be done the night before. If your operation is planned for later in the day, the preoperative cleaning can be done that morning, depending on your surgeon's preference.

There may still be delays at this stage, which can be vexing when you have psychologically prepared yourself to be operated on at a certain time. There are many reasons a delay could occur—an earlier operation that took longer than scheduled, a shortage of ancillary staff, et cetera. The operation requires coordination of a number of different elements, and your surgeon will not want you to be anesthetized until everything is in place, so that your surgery will go as quickly and smoothly as possible. It's best to be prepared for this possibility, and if it should happen, simply to not let it upset you.

Prior to surgery, you will be given a tranquilizer, such as Valium, to keep you calm and relaxed and you will be placed on a stretcher to be wheeled into the operating room (referred to as the OR).

Before being placed on the operating table, you will have electrodes—like those for the ECG—attached to your back to provide information about your heart's electrical activity during the operation. You will feel a momentary sharp pinprick (much as you would when a blood sample is taken) when the local anesthetic is administered before the intravenous drip attachments (IVs) are put in place in the veins of both arms or wrists. The intravenous drips are used to provide you with glucose and with saline solution to maintain body fluid and electrolytes. The anesthesiologist will also use the IV lines to maintain the correct levels of anesthetizing agents, as well as to administer the anticoagulant heparin, and later the procoagulant protamine. One of the IV lines is threaded up the vein until it reaches the vena cava, the large vein entering the heart. This allows the anesthesiologist to administer medication directly to the heart.

Following administration of a local or general anesthetic, a catheter may be inserted into the jugular vein in the side of the neck and guided into the right side of the heart. This is the Swan-Ganz, or balloon, catheter.

When it is inside the right atrium, a balloon at the tip is slightly inflated and the blood carries the catheter and balloon into the lungs. The blood's pressure in the pulmonary artery provides an extremely accurate reading of how well the heart is working. This catheter can also help to check the cardiac output (how much blood the heart is circulating). A small amount of cold solution is injected into the heart and tested for by a temperature probe on the catheter tip. If there is a slight overall temperature change, the blood is circulating well because the cold solution has been diluted with the total moving volume of blood.

Still another IV line is placed in the radial artery in the wrist, where it can measure the arterial blood pressure and the gas composition of the blood. The gas composition is carefully watched to make sure that the ratio of carbon dioxide to oxygen is stable.

A Foley catheter is also passed through the urethra and into the bladder. (In men, the catheter is passed up the opening at the tip of the penis. In women, it is inserted directly into the urethra.) Its purpose is to drain the urine, which collects in a calibrated bag. This allows the anesthesiologist to know how well the kidneys are functioning. Some people dread the thought of a urinary catheter, but its insertion is only mildly discomforting, and done after the patient is fully asleep.

All the while that the various tubes are being put in place, the anesthesiologist is gradually adding a mixture of drugs to one of the IV units. One of these, Fentanyl, is a powerful narcotic analgesic (blocker of pain) that causes drowsiness and then unconsciousness. Another drug causes temporary amnesia. Before it was used, patients sometimes recalled what had happened to them during the operation, even though they had appeared to be unconscious at the time. A muscle relaxant, such as pancuronium, is also given to prevent the patient from twitching or moving during the operation. (Contrary to popular belief, a gas anesthetic such as nitrous oxide is rarely used for coronary bypass operations.) Throughout the operation, the anesthesiologist will monitor the patient's vital signs and give additional doses of the various medications as needed.

Once the patient is "induced" into a semiconscious, pain-free state, the endotracheal tube is inserted into place. First a laryngoscope is inserted past the tongue and into the throat to allow the anesthesiologist to watch the passage of the endotracheal tube between the vocal chords. The endotracheal tube is then quickly slid down and the balloon at its end inflated to hold it securely in place. The endotracheal tube connects to the respirator, which does the work of breathing for the patient. When you wake up in the recovery room, the endotracheal tube will still be in place and will be there until you are ready to start breathing on your own again. It prevents you from speaking and your throat will also be a little sore from having a foreign object lodged inside it. This irritation disappears shortly after you are "extubated," when the tube is removed.

A nasogastric tube may also be inserted at this time. This tube is passed through the nostril, and then into the stomach via the esophagus. Its purpose is to siphon off digestive juices that might otherwise collect and cause nausea.

The patient is swabbed with an antiseptic solution like Betadine one more time, and the surgery is at last ready to begin. While one surgeon and his or her assistants work on opening up the chest, another team will be busy working on the patient's leg(s) to remove the saphenous veins. Lines are drawn along the site of incision with a marker, and the procedure commences. There is little bleeding, for the surgeons continuously cauterize the blood vessels with an instrument that is tipped with a thin, heated wire.

When the surgeon working on the chest has to divide the breastbone, a sawlike instrument is used. This is very much like the saw that is used to remove plaster casts; it cleaves through the breastbone rapidly but does not hurt soft tissue. A series of graded retractors are then placed and the chest is slowly opened. This is done very gradually to minimize injury to the surrounding tissue. When the two parts of the breastbone are about eight to ten centimeters apart, the surgeon can begin working on the interior cavity itself.

If one or both of the internal mammary arteries is to be used, this is the time when it is painstakingly removed from the chest wall together with the tissue that provides it with support, the pedicle. Otherwise, the surgeon proceeds straight to work on the heart. After first dividing the fat that lies underneath the breastbone, the surgeon gently moves the lungs aside preparatory to incising the pericardium, the tough sac that protects the heart. The living, pulsating heart is now open to view. The surgeon examines the heart carefully, looking for any white, mottled patches that would indicate muscle damage.[1]

By now, the saphenous vein (or sometimes, veins) have been removed. For each bypass, about twenty centimeters (about eight inches) is needed. The vein

1. Note: Since the heart is not actually cut into during coronary bypass surgery, strictly speaking the operation is not "open-heart surgery."

has also been filled with saline solution to check that there are no leaks and that the valves are not blocked, and that quality is adequate.

The surgeon then takes a cannula—a hollow plastic tube with one end sharpened on the diagonal and the other temporarily sealed with a clamp—and inserts it into the aorta. A plastic tube connecting to the heart-lung machine is primed with saline solution and attached to the still-sealed end of the cannula. The surgeon carefully checks that there are no air bubbles in the plastic tube or between it and the aortic cannula. Since this is aortic blood that will be routed into the body, any air bubbles could cause a devastating embolism. Next, another cannula is inserted into the right atrium.

Once both cannulas are in place and are connected to the heart-lung machine, the heart is placed on partial bypass. This means that the heart continues to beat, but its function is taken over by the machine. Partial bypass allows the surgeons to check that the heart-lung machine is performing satisfactorily. Also, since the heart shrinks in size when it is stopped, the surgeons want to first check what the correct length should be for the new bypass conduit. At this time, the surgeons may inject a vasodilator into the internal mammary artery to open it up (if this vessel is being used).

The heart is then stilled by direct injection of a solution of cold potassium cardioplegic fluid into the coronary arteries. The surgeon can then begin the meticulous work of stitching the new vessels into place. If the mammary artery is being used, only one end usually needs to be attached (although "free grafts" of the mammary artery are sometimes performed). If the saphenous vein is being used, one end is carefully sewn around a hole punctured in the aorta; then the opposite end is attached to the coronary artery. While the by-passing vessels are being stitched into place, cardioplegic fluid continues to be pumped into the coronary arteries intermittently to keep the heart still and the body tem-perature low. The stitching of the vessels is where the surgeons' delicacy and skill come most into play, since this task determines the viability of the new blood vessels. (See diagram.)

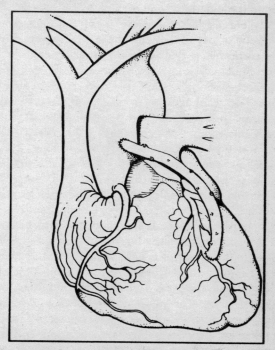

Once the bypassing vessels are firmly in place, the blood is allowed to warm up and the heart usually starts beating again by itself. Occasionally, the surgeon will need to give the heart an electric shock to start it up again. The heart can then be taken off bypass, the retractors removed, and the breastbone wired in place to knit together. The incision in the chest, which had been open shortly before, is now ready to be stitched together. The body's recuperating powers are such that the spliced skin and tissue quickly grow back together again, leaving only the narrow chest scar that is heart surgery's trademark.

CHAPTER 6

The Recovery Period

Following the surgery, you will be taken to the intensive care unit, usually referred to as the ICU. This ward is equipped with highly sophisticated monitors that record all your vital signs: your blood pressure, temperature, oxygen and carbon dioxide levels, and the heart's electrical activity. Here, you will be monitored around the clock by nurses who have been trained in the special care needed by patients who have just had surgery.

It is normal to have a very slow heartbeat after heart surgery, and patients are routinely fitted with a temporary pacemaker to stimulate electrical activity. A small box that is taped to your chest, the pacemaker connects to wires directly attached to your heart. (These wires provide immediate electrical access to the heart; once your condition has stabilized, your physician can remove them harmlessly and painlessly.) The pacemaker serves to supplement the actions of the heart's own pacemakers in the sinoatrial nodes; as your heartbeat returns to normal, the pacemaker "kicks in" less and less often. It is usually removed after one or two days, although the wires are left in for five to ten days.

When you first arrive at the ICU, you will still be very groggy from the anesthetic. You may also feel thirsty from the diuretic effect of some of the medications given during the operation. Another common complaint in the ICU is a feeling of being very cold. Your body was cooled down considerably during the operation to reduce its need for nutrients, and the warming-up process may take a while, even though the room temperature of the unit is quite comfortable. A tendency to feel cold can also be a side effect of the anesthetic, which blocks the shivering response that might warm you up. The ICU nurses are aware of this problem and will supply you with a blanket to make sure you are kept warm. If you tend to feel cold easily and have poor peripheral circulation, it's a good idea to mention this to one of the doctors who interview you before the operation.

Your sense of time will also be distorted as you drift in and out of wakefulness. Hours may seem like minutes and vice versa. Patients are also often frustrated by their inability to communicate with the nurses, since the combination of drugs and the endotracheal tube prevents you from talking at this time. The main thing to remember is that the nurses in the ICU are well trained, skilled in nonverbal communication, and are constantly watching to make sure that you are comfortable and recovering according to schedule. To ease the communication problem, the nurses will ask you to use hand signals and word boards to check on your needs.

After a few hours, your family will probably be allowed to come and visit. You will be able to hear their voices, and the touch of a loved one's hand at this moment can be very soothing. However, you will probably be too weak to communicate much with them at this point, and in any case, the endotracheal tube makes speaking impossible.

The doctor or ICU nurse will usually try to prepare the family as to what to expect, because the first sight of a loved one in a hospital bed surrounded by tubes and monitors can be alarming. Family members should try not to become upset, and perhaps more importantly, not to pass their alarm on to the patient. The human body is able to recover remarkably fast, and most bypass patients are out of the ICU in one to three days. The same patient who may have looked to the untrained eye to be in pretty bad shape immediately after the operation will very likely be taking his or her first steps out of bed with the help of a nurse or spouse two to three days later.

Occasionally, patients will have a setback or be slower than usual in recovering from the anesthesia, and the physician will want them to stay longer in the ICU for closer monitoring. Any check to your recovery can be alarming, especially when a monitor loudly beeps to signal that there is a problem. A small percentage of bypass patients[1] experience some form of setback, but these can usually be overcome within a short time and, of course, the ICU is the ward best equipped and staffed to deal with any such problem.

Among the complications that arise following the surgery are infections or bleeding around the site of the chest and leg incisions, palpitations and other heart-

---

1. The likelihood of setbacks varies according to the overall health of the patient and the severity of his or her heart disease.

rhythm or electrical abnormalities, and fluid buildup in the lungs. More serious adverse reactions—such as stroke, heart attacks, and kidney failure—do occur, but only in a very few patients and the number is dropping every year with the increasing sophistication of surgeons and equipment.

The majority of complications can be quickly dealt with. Infections respond to antibiotics; palpitations and fibrillation may require additional drugs or an electric charge administered via the wires that remain in the patient's chest. Fibrillation—which may feel as if horses are galloping inside your chest—can be scary. It is normal to have some fibrillation or palpitations during the first few days following surgery. (Note: If fibrillation occurs after you have left the hospital, call your doctor.) Again, it is important to keep in mind that more than ninety-nine percent of all routine bypass patients do recover fully from their operations.

Lying on your back in the ICU, you can easily let your imagination get the better of you. In *The Heart Surgery Handbook,* Carol Cohan and her co-authors describe how one patient became convinced she was going to die. She had overheard a nurse say that she was "in failure." It was not until another nurse explained to her that this was shorthand for "congestive heart failure," and that this was a condition that can easily be treated by draining the fluid buildup in the lungs, that she realized she would be fine.

As you begin your return to consciousness following the operation, you will feel some discomfort in the chest and possibly the legs. You may also feel some friction from the chest tubes or the IV lines in your wrists. It is also possible that your hands will be lightly restrained with tape to prevent you from accidentally disconnecting any of the tubes while you are still groggy. (Note: Provided there are no complications, chest tubes are usually removed after two days, the endotracheal tube after less than one day, and the Foley catheter and IVs after three to four days.)

You may also find the endotracheal tube an annoyance, although it should not be causing you any pain. This tube connects to a respirator, which does your breathing for you. If you try to breathe *against* the flow of the respirator, you may feel as if you are not getting any air. Do not panic. All you have to do is relax and the respirator will continue supplying you with all the oxygen you need; there is absolutely no risk of suffocating while on a respirator.

The respirators are designed to allow you to start breathing on your own as you regain strength. An occasional beep serves to remind you that you need to take a breath, and the nurses in the room will keep you fully informed as to how to use the respirator.

Sometimes patients become used to the respirator and are afraid when it comes time to have it removed. Again, relaxing makes the process easier. The nurses and doctors know what they are doing and will not remove the tube too early. The tube takes only seconds to remove, and it should come out with little discomfort. There will also be oxygen at hand to help you breathe regularly once the endotracheal tube is out. There is no risk to the procedure, and staying calm and following the respiratory therapist's instructions are the best way to ensure that you will feel comfortable breathing on your own again.

From the ICU, you will be moved to a step-down unit, which is also referred to as the recovery room. There is not as much intense activity in the recovery room, but you will still be watched by nurses twenty-four hours a day and a physician will look in on you every half hour or so. You will have your blood pressure taken every two hours, an ECG monitor will be kept in place, the oxygen levels in your blood will be constantly monitored via an IV in the radial (wrist) artery, and you will have daily chest X-rays to determine if both lungs are functioning and are not becoming filled with fluid. You will also usually be allowed to sit on the edge of your bed for brief periods to get you used to moving around a little.

Physical therapy will also be begun during your recovery-room stay, and will continue afterward in the general ward. You will be encouraged to cough while "splinting" your chest to remove fluid from your lungs and bronchi. You will also be given an incentive spirometer—an instrument you blow into as hard as you can, a small plastic ball indicating your progress. These activities can be uncomfortable at first (particularly if you have been a heavy smoker), but are necessary to bring your breathing back to normal.

At one time, it was thought that the longer a patient rested and stayed immobile following an operation, the better. The contemporary attitude is that a rapid return to independence results in a speedier recovery. As you grow stronger, your nurses will encourage you to do more and more on your own while still monitoring you carefully. When it is time for you to leave the recovery room, you will be taken to a private or semiprivate room, or to a special "telemetry" bed on the general ward. You will still have nurses checking in on you frequently, but there is obviously not the same round-the-clock attention.

Now that you have moved to your new room, you

may be wondering what would happen if you were to
have a problem when a nurse is not immediately in the
area. You need not worry that you are being neglected.
The ECG machine, to which you are still attached,
connects with a computer that would instantly alert the
hospital staff at the first abnormal sign. (Note: The ECG
monitor will often beep if you make a sudden move-
ment or cough. You will soon get used to this occasional
beeping, which is not a signal of anything to worry
about.) Your blood oxygen levels will continue to be
monitored, and the monitor is similarly connected to a
computer. The nurses will make sure that your return
to independence is not hastier than you can handle, and
they will be present every time you need to get out of
bed.

The Foley catheter will now be removed (if this was
not already done in the recovery room). Men in particular may feel a slight burning sensation the first few
times they urinate. You can help ease this irritation by
drinking lots of fluids, which is to be encouraged as it
promotes healing in general.

You may also find it difficult or even frightening to
go to the bathroom by yourself, and because of the
body's inactivity while being bedridden, you could be
constipated at this time. The nurses will provide you
with a suppository or mineral oil (which is taken orally)
to help loosen the stool and make bowel movements
less of a strain.

The phases of your recovery are carefully watched by
the hospital staff, who "step down" the amount of care
you are given as your health improves. The next stage
of your recovery is very much in your own hands. Your
nurses and doctors will start encouraging you to move

around, at first with some help and then by yourself. Even a short walk to the nurses' station and back to your room may seem taxing. You will be tired and probably experiencing some pain in your legs and chest. You may also be worried about putting a strain on your heart—a worry which is unfounded, since your heart will be getting a better supply of oxygen now than it did before the operation.

It is vital that you overcome your reluctance or discomfort and follow the exercise program your doctors recommend. Recent studies have shown that even healthy volunteers who are confined to bed for several weeks suffer a depressed immune system, poor circulation, and loss of muscle tone. Hence the importance of moving around as soon as you can. Although exerting yourself may be unpleasant at some times, you will soon be able to feel its rewards as your strength starts to rebound. You might even find yourself enjoying the challenge of making slight increases in the distance you walk each day.

Sometimes you may feel as if you are being hurried along too quickly, being asked to recover faster than you are able. Most of the pushing that the hospital staff does is for your own benefit, intended to encourage you not to become too reliant on pain medication, as well as to overcome a natural reluctance to move around when you're feeling weak. If you really do feel neglected, ask to talk to your doctor about it. He or she can help you decide what is too much activity for you, and can explain any phasing down of your pain medication.

After a week to ten days, you will probably be ready to go home again. (This can be longer if you had complications or if you will be flying a long distance.) While this is a wonderful moment, it is also a difficult one. At home, you and your family will be responsible for all your care, including making sure you take the right medicines at the right time. Hospitals generally have special discharge classes or videotapes to help you cope with this next stage. You will not be expected to handle your emergence from the comforting hospital environment without any lifeline. Most hospitals have a special number you can call when you have any questions on recovering from cardiac surgery. You should also make sure that you are in regular touch with your personal cardiologist and surgeon.

Being surrounded by the familiar objects and spaces of home can be comforting, but it can also make you realize how weak you are. In the first few weeks after surgery, you can expect to become fatigued very easily, even doing just the day-to-day tasks that you would normally not even have given a thought to. The tiredness that follows surgery is different from the usual sort of tiredness that might follow a busy day. It tends to come on extremely suddenly: one moment you feel fine, the next you feel utterly exhausted. The only way to combat this sudden exhaustion is to rest before you get tired, but this is hard to do. Try to spread your activities throughout the day, with plenty of free time to rest in between. You may at first want to ask friends and relatives to call or visit only at certain hours. Even a phone call can be emotionally and physically fatiguing.

The loss of energy that follows surgery improves with each passing week. Some people feel fully recovered and better than ever before in two to three months; for others, it may take longer. One thing that everyone can expect—and which can be disheartening—is that days when you feel your recovery is progressing wonderfully can often be followed by days when you feel worse again, as if you have regressed. This is perfectly normal, and you should try not to add to the frustration by fretting about it. These periods of regression are usually a sign that you were trying to do too much too soon. You should continue to make sure you do some exercise and keep up your interests, but take things a little more slowly and don't rush to do more, even if you feel you can handle it at the time.

Arthur, a sixty-seven-year-old retired businessman, had a successful triple bypass. He was home within a week and, aside from some palpitations in the first few days following the operation, was free of any side effects. Everything had gone well physically, but emotionally Arthur was a changed man. He no longer bothered to read the newspaper or watch the evening news. He ignored the latest book by his favorite mystery writer that his wife had bought him as a coming-home present. And even being with his three-year-old grandson, with whom he had earlier established a special relationship, was "just too tiring."

Although Arthur's cardiologist had checked him out and said he would soon be fit enough to start playing golf again, he spent his days listlessly sitting in an armchair or sleeping. It was not until a friend who had had bypass surgery a year before told Arthur about his depression that Arthur realized what the problem was and started to deal with it.

Transient depression is an occasional side effect of bypass surgery, and one that is often insufficiently recognized and prepared for. It can last a few days or for months after the operation, and it affects not only the quality of life but the patient's health and perception of his or her recovery. Depression can be particularly severe for patients who have suffered a recent loss or who have any history of psychological problems, but it can also affect people who have been emotionally stable in the past.

It is easier for both you and your family to cope with bouts of depression if you are aware that it is, by and large, a normal part of the recovery process. You can expect that there will be some mental and emotional changes immediately after the operation and in the months following it. You may suddenly find yourself bursting into tears for no reason at all (which can be disconcerting for those accustomed to keeping a tight rein on their emotions), suffering from a feeling of hopelessness or worthlessness, or feeling incredibly angry toward everybody and everything around you. Such feelings or reactions generally pass quickly, and it is important for you to remember that they *are* temporary and will disappear as you regain your strength.

There are several reasons why heart surgery patients are prone to depression, emotional lability (a tendency to weep easily), or anger. There may be an as yet not fully understood organic explanation, resulting from a combination of anesthesia, hypothermia, and time spent on the heart-lung machine. Another cause might be the disorientation experienced in the intensive care unit: a place that is often noisy and always intensely lit, making it difficult to distinguish between day and night. For many people, too, this may be their first real confrontation with their own mortality. And finally, there is the disconcerting experience of being absolutely in the hands of others, unable to care for oneself, during the early recovery period. People who have always felt in control of their lives and who are used to being independent, often find this intense period of dependence particularly vexing.

In the early stages of recovery, you might find yourself disoriented by the strange environment and by the aftereffects of the anesthesia. Loss of memory, particularly about the operation day, and brief spells of amnesia are common at this time. Some people may even experience mild hallucinations or paranoia—one patient, for example, was convinced for several hours that he was in a concentration camp. It may be that this happens more often than patients admit to their doctors, since people may feel ashamed of their "crazy notions." The important point to remember is that you were not going crazy, that the hallucinations were a very temporary effect of physical and environmental changes, and that other patients share your experience.

During the step-down phase of recovery in the general ward and/or private rooms, there are other, subtler mental adjustments taking place. Now that your operation is safely behind you, you are no longer struggling to survive but have time to contemplate both your condition and your fears. Your emotions may veer from euphoria at the awareness of surviving the operation and feeling your strength coming back to anger or a feeling of worthlessness and hopelessness. Small events —a nurse who seems a little brusque, a visitor who arrives a few minutes late—assume significance out of all proportion.

Again, it is helpful to confront the reasons why you may be having "irrational" mood swings. Try to talk over your feelings with a family member, a nurse, or one of the hospital counselors. Most people who have undergone bypass surgery have an emotional response to the operation, and it is reasonable to do so. Your body has undergone considerable physical trauma, your heart was stopped, you're uncomfortable, and you constantly have to rely on other people for your needs. It is little wonder that this is a time of questioning and anxiety.

The return-home period sees a (usually) milder form of the same mood swings. The process of recovery, both mental and physical, requires work. Patients may dwell on the details of their operation over and over again, trying to come to terms with this major event in their lives. Returning to one's old interests at this time is difficult too. You know that your operation was the result of your way of life . . . so how can you just plunge back into your old life? The moments of weakness are frustrating, and setbacks (which are common but usually don't last long) can plunge one into despair by graphically revealing the reality of one's own mortality.

Remember that all of this is normal. Being open about your feelings and fears and accepting that these are part of the work of getting back your health can make all the difference. If you don't have someone close to you to discuss things with—or are reluctant to burden a family member with feelings you yourself haven't yet come to grips with—you may wish to contact a professional counselor (perhaps through the hospital), a local branch of the American Heart Association, or friends who have undergone the operation themselves. This is a natural part of your healing process and should never be thought of as a sign of weakness or personal failure.

The postoperative period can be a painful one for

family members as well. Not only do they have to confront their own feelings about mortality and potential loss, but they have the spectacle of a loved one in pain or reduced to uncharacteristic helplessness. The reaction can sometimes be one of anger or irritability toward the patient. The patient's need to talk about the operation, slow recovery, and lassitude can all be very trying. Family members should be encouraged as much as possible to understand both what the operation and the recovery period entail, and what their own and the patient's psychological reactions may be. You may wish to encourage your spouse or other family members to attend the patient education programs provided by the hospital, or to read more about the operation and its psychological side.

Shortly after you return home you can begin a gradual return to your normal way of life. The hospital staff will advise you which activities you should avoid during the first few months after the surgery. For example, you will be warned against driving a car for the three to six weeks it takes for your chest to heal, due to the risk of hitting the steering wheel in an accident. (It is okay to ride in a car as a passenger.) Also, any activity that might raise blood pressure—such as lifting a heavy object—is better left alone during the first few weeks.

Many patients worry about how surgery will affect their sex lives. They may be concerned that sex could put too much strain on their hearts and cause a heart attack. They might be worried that the chest and leg scars could make them unattractive. They may fear that their bodies have changed in some unknown way, or have gotten used to thinking of themselves as invalids.

There is, in fact, no reason that people who were appropriate bypass candidates should not be able to return to a fuller and more active sex life after the operation. Bypass increases the heart's ability to function, and thus provides better blood flow to the rest of the body and a decreased risk of heart attack. Like most fears, those concerning sex are best talked about—both with your partner and with your cardiologist.

Returning to an active sex life should be a gradual process. For the first month or so, you are best advised to avoid anything strenuous, including orgasm . . . not because your heart cannot cope, but because your body needs all its energy to recover from the trauma of being operated upon. You will probably not feel like having sex at this time, anyway, both because of the discomfort of the incisions and strained muscles and because your sex drive is likely to be depressed initially.

It is natural for both you and your partner to feel anxious at first, and anxiety is an antiaphrodisiac. Start out slowly and try to create an atmosphere that is most comfortable for both of you. You may wish to voice your concerns to each other—after all, your partner may be fearful of hurting you. You can feel reassured that if you are able to climb a flight of stairs without palpitations and pain, you should be able to withstand the physical exertion of intercourse with no problem.

If lack of desire or impotence persists, don't hesitate to contact your physician. Some people feel shy talking about sex with a doctor, but it is part of your health and part of the doctor's job. Some of the medications that you might be taking can have impotence as a side effect. It is often possible to adjust the dose or try a related drug to deal with this problem. Remember, there is no such thing as a silly question if it's something that worries you.

Returning to an active sexual and physical life after a bypass operation is certainly within most people's reach, as the following case history demonstrates:

Mary, a thirty-one-year-old trial lawyer, was recovering from a quadruple bypass operation. A number of her family members had died prematurely of heart disease, and Mary's first concern had been survival when hospitalization—following a visit to her doctor for unusual chest pains—led to diagnosis of severe coronary artery disease. After being operated on successfully without complication, she found her anxieties focused on whether she would be able to lead a life that was normal for someone her age. She had recently been married, and she was afraid that now she might never be able to have children . . . a worry that was in the back of her mind all the time and that began to put a strain on her relationship with her husband.

Mary's cardiologist and surgeon reassured her that there was no reason she could not become pregnant and have a normal delivery. She was delighted over this news. She subsequently gave birth to two healthy children over the next four years.

Another question you may be wondering about is how soon you can return to work after the operation. Sometimes people fear that they either won't be able to go back to work at all or that they will not have the energy to perform their jobs as well as they formerly did. (This is particularly true of people who decided to have a bypass operation following a heart attack.) Again, the bypass operation should raise your energy level and lower your risk of heart attack, so returning to work should not be an obstacle. Indeed, most patients have successfully gone back to their old jobs and even on to new ones.

You do need to ease into things, however, and not leap straight into a hectic schedule. Even if you feel fine a few weeks after the operation, try to pace your workload so you have some time to rest. As you continue to regain strength, you can gauge your energies to be as productive as you want to be. But be careful not to let a demanding work schedule become an excuse to go back to unhealthful eating and exercise habits.

Not so very long ago doctors advised heart patients to retire early and to lead as leisurely a life as possible. This is now recognized as being poor advice: people who retain a vigorous interest in a rewarding profession and who have responsibilities tend to be fitter and have a greater sense of self-worth than those who feel their infirmity has caused them to withdraw from life. Stress and activity are not synonymous; a busy, fulfilling life is often a healthier one.

Interestingly enough, a 1983 study that was part of the Seattle Heart Watch found that as many or more bypass patients retired when compared with similar patients treated with medication. Ironically, this was *in spite of* the finding that the bypass patients had a greater capacity for work (as measured on a stress ECG). Although some detractors of the bypass operation may see the high retirement rate as a sign of failure, the explanation lies elsewhere. When the study's authors delved deeper into the mystery, they found that the reasons for retirement were largely societal and psychological.

On the psychological side, patients tend to blame "stress on the job" for their heart disease and were encouraged to think this way by their physicians. Others saw the surgery as a reason to reexamine their lives and to break away from a boring or unstimulating routine.

Outside society tended to regard the bypass patients as invalids and to treat them as such. (This has since changed considerably as the operation has become more common.) Employers were less inclined to hire or re-hire someone who had had surgery—particularly since they feared the massive increases in workers' disability premiums if someone suffered a cardiac event on the job. And, finally, patients who retired were often as well or better off financially through a combination of disability payments, pension, and Social Security than if they continued to work.

Today, bypass surgery is more routine and employers are not likely to attach a stigma to it. It may be useful to explain the surgery to your employer before-hand. After all, the surgery is designed to make you more efficient, not less.

CHAPTER 7

Special Situations

The standard profile of the bypass candidate is of a man in his late sixties who is having the operation for the first time. Advances in operative technique, in myocardial preservation, and in the thinking of cardiothoracic surgeons have greatly expanded the range of patients whose health can benefit from bypass surgery. According to the chairman of the American Heart Association's Council on Cardiovascular Surgery, "The patient population as a whole is sicker, older, and has more of what the insurance companies call 'outlying factors.'"

More and more often, bypass candidates may be women, diabetics, and elderly, or patients who have had several prior angioplasties or a previous bypass operation. An important factor for the successful outcome of these operations is the choice of the surgical team and of the medical center. Experience counts, and the more of these particular types of operation a team has performed, the better they are able to cope with or avoid complications. The availability of ancillary per-

sonnel—endocrinologists for diabetics, geriatric specialists for older patients—can also help to ensure that the
operation will be a success. These new trends are certainly good for cardiac patients who may once have
thought—or been advised by their physicians—that their
condition, age, or sex precluded them from the benefits
of bypass surgery.

Women

---

*Jane, a forty-seven-year-old advertising executive,
had been experiencing frequent chest pains, particularly at stressful times during the workday. She tried to
dismiss the pains as being from indigestion, but they
grew so severe that she made time in her busy schedule
to visit her doctor. To her amazement, her physician
urged her to have an angiogram, as her electrocardiograms were abnormal and there was a family history of
premature death from cardiovascular disease.*

*Jane's angiogram showed extensive coronary artery
disease, and she subsequently had a triple bypass operation. The operation was performed without complications, and Jane found herself back at work a month
later, her energy renewed and her chest pains a thing
of the past.*

Of the 320,000 coronary bypass operations performed
in 1988, 88,000 (twenty-eight percent) of the patients
were women. Most of the studies on bypass surgery—
and, indeed, of heart disease in general—have focused
primarily or exclusively on men, but there is no reason
to believe that the surgery is any less advantageous to
women with coronary artery disease.

An early study that included women, the CASS registry, found that they tended to have slightly higher mortality rates and more complications than men. The prevailing theory has been that women's smaller body size and smaller coronary arteries are the explanation for this. Another possible cause is that the women who were being operated on in the late nineteen seventies (the time of the CASS study) were predominantly at a more advanced stage of coronary disease. There are several grounds for believing this might be the case. Women appear to be less inclined to seek diagnosis and treatment at an early stage of coronary artery disease, and there is some evidence that ischemic attacks in women are more often "silent" than in men. (It may be that women still think of heart disease as a man's ailment and are more likely to ignore chest pain as being due to some other cause.) The result was that women (and, in many cases, their physicians as well) were less liable both to recognize the problem and to consider a surgical option.

The number of women who have bypass surgery has been steadily rising, and today's results for women are very much on par with the excellent results for men (although no long-term study has as yet been instituted to confirm this). Surgeons are also using internal mammary artery grafts on women patients more often than in the past, with correspondingly better patency rates (the length of time the new vessels stay unblocked). The rising percentage of women bypass patients also means that cardiothoracic surgeons (and anesthesiologists) are getting more experience in operating on people of smaller body size and with smaller coronary arteries. Any woman who is diagnosed as having coronary artery disease should certainly consider bypass surgery as a viable option and should not be overly concerned that she is an unusual or high-risk patient, since this no longer the case. Remember, cardiovascular disease is the number-one killer of women as well as of men, and many of these deaths could be prevented by prompt, appropriate medical care.

If you are a woman over the age of fifty-five, you should insist on an ECG as part of your annual checkup. This is particularly imperative if you are 1) postmenopausal, 2) a cigarette smoker, 3) a long-term user of oral contraceptives, or 4) twenty pounds or more overweight.

Reoperations

When Harry's angiogram showed more than eighty percent blockage both in his left anterior descending artery and in two places in the right coronary artery, he agreed without hesitation to a bypass operation. The 297-pound lawyer was confident that he would get through surgery with little difficulty and that it would substantially benefit his health. After all, he had already had the operation once before.

The number of patients having bypass surgery for the second time around is steadily increasing. This is hardly surprising when one considers that upward of five hundred thousand Americans had had bypass surgery by the year 1980. Since some of the grafts cannot stay open after seven to twelve years, the majority of these earlier patients are liable once again to be afflicted by the ischemic episodes that required them to have the operation in the first place. Many of them may be excellent candidates for a "reop."

Reoperations are technically a little more difficult than first-time bypass operations. The surgery takes longer because there is scar tissue at the site of the chest incision to be cut through, but it is generally not necessary for reop patients to be on the heart-lung machine longer than other patients. One major question is whether the patient will have sufficiently viable veins for the grafts, and this is usually something the surgeon can determine before even suggesting surgery. It was more common for earlier bypass operations to consist of a single or double graft, and use of the internal mammary artery was fairly rare. In most cases considered for reoperation, some of the saphenous veins and both internal mammary arteries are usually still intact and can be used for revascularization during the second procedure.

Reoperations are ideally conducted by the original surgeon, who knows the patient's heart from the inside. When this is not possible, the current surgeon will seek to obtain the records from the first operation and will also try to speak to the original surgeon.

As for Harry, he was ready to go home a week after his second bypass operation. He barely noticed the pain in his leg incisions, since he knew from experience that it would quickly pass and he would be able to return to his active life-style. His stay in the recovery room seemed much easier this time around, because he knew just what to expect and had few fears and apprehensions. In fact, his overriding feeling was of relief, euphoria, and privilege. After all, it's not everyone who can say he has twice been given a second lease on life.

The Elderly

Max, an eighty-five-year-old retired philosophy professor, reluctantly agreed to his cardiologist's suggestion that he have a bypass operation. For the past several years, Max's activities had been severely curtailed by angina pains and breathlessness. Even climbing the short flight of stairs to his study had become too much for him, and he had had to delay work on his partially written new book—which he now feared he would never finish. Max's tests had shown that his heart was still strong, his left ventricle still contracting powerfully, and his general health was that of a much younger man. However, he had extensive blockages in two of his coronary arteries, and a small blockage in a third. Max understood the need for his operation but thought he was too old. His secret fear was that he would not leave the operating table alive.

After meeting with both the cardiothoracic surgeon and the hospital's gerontological specialist, Max agreed to surgery. The operation went without a hitch, but he had to stay in the hospital room for an extra week while an infection in his leg incision was treated. Six weeks after the surgery, Max was back at work on his book, which he felt confident would be his best yet.

As the number of older people in this country has steadily climbed, the social and medical attitudes toward the elderly population have also been undergoing change. Doctors are less reluctant to recommend major surgery for patients in their seventies and eighties, and these patients feel more confident about a successful outcome of such treatment. There are, of course, some special considerations to be taken into account in balancing the risks of the surgery with its benefits. Older patients have a slightly higher mortality and complication rate than younger angina patients. But the mortality rate is still quite low (approximately five percent) and the operation's value in terms of pain relief, renewed activity levels, and increased lifespan is immense and like that for younger patients.

Before agreeing to any major operation, the elderly person should appraise both his or her own general health and how well the hospital is equipped to deal with older patients. Many hospitals now have gerontological units whose staff are trained to watch for complications specific to this population group—such as adverse reactions to medication, which can occur at a lower dose in older persons. The gerontological unit can be asked to consult with the surgeon and the patient to help weigh the decision, and they will generally follow the patient's progress of treatment. This may be particularly of value during the period of follow-up care: as a result, older patients are often slower to recover, spend more time in the ICU, and seem more likely to become disoriented postoperatively. The assistance of an ancillary gerontological unit can be invaluable in smoothing out any difficulties during this period.

Coronary artery bypass surgery has been found to be efficacious in relieving pain and silent ischemia in patients of all ages. "As far as we know, there is no upper limit," reports a prominent cardiologist. There is no reason for an individual over the age of seventy-five who has crippling angina not to consider surgical relief as a possible option.

Diabetics

People with juvenile onset diabetes (also called Type I or insulin-dependent diabetes) are susceptible to a variety of cardiovascular disorders at a considerably earlier age than the general population. In many cases, coronary bypass surgery can provide relief to diabetics with occluded coronary arteries, but the mortality and complication rate is higher than for the general population and the operation is not always appropriate. Bypass surgery is further complicated for diabetics if there is diffuse disease of the distal sections of the coronary arteries, or if there is evidence that the diabetic condition has severely damaged the leg veins and/or the kidney's blood vessels.

Physicians will select out diabetic bypass patients very carefully to avoid the risk of complications that might outweigh the surgical benefits, but there is still a somewhat elevated mortality rate for these patients. Although the mortality rate is high when compared with the average bypass patient, a success rate of ninety percent or greater is an impressive achievement for such a high-risk group. Juvenile onset diabetics with severe angina should not dismiss bypass surgery out of hand, since it does offer tremendous advantages and the odds are not all that bad. They should nevertheless be aware of the increased risk that is part of the equation when making their decision whether to have the surgery or not.

Since a raised cholesterol level seems to go hand in hand with diabetes, it is even more urgent that diabetics (whether or not they have angina, are contemplating a bypass operation, or have had one) take strong measures to lower their dietary intake of animal fats and cholesterol. Careful monitoring of blood glucose levels and insulin intake is vital for diabetics to maintain their health in general, and may very well reduce the risk of developing atherosclerosis.

Adult onset (Type II or insulin-independent) diabetes is a less severe illness and does not play as insidious a role in the development of atherosclerosis. This disorder can usually be kept in control by losing weight, eating a low-fat, low-calorie diet, and exercising regularly . . . all of which profit the health of the individual's heart as well.

CHAPTER 8

Alternative Treatments: Pros and Cons

Depending on the degree of your coronary artery disease and the extent to which it either interferes with your life-style or endangers your health, you and your doctor may decide to pursue a medical course of treatment and, possibly, less invasive procedures.

Medical maintenance is usually recommended for patients who have stable angina, who have blockages of fifty percent or less of only one artery (other than the left main branch), or who have other medical conditions (such as kidney disease) that would make them potentially high-risk candidates for bypass surgery. There are gray areas, of course, and sometimes your physician will suggest trying a period of medical treatment as a stopgap before bypass surgery.

The purpose of medical maintenance is principally to

stop or slow deterioration of the coronary arteries, to alleviate the pain of angina, and to minimize the possibility of myocardial infarctions (heart attacks). An assortment of drugs with a variety of therapeutic effects may be called for: some to lower blood pressure, others to reduce serum cholesterol levels, still others to improve the heart's efficiency and help prevent heart attacks, and some to stop blood clots from forming. All of these medications have to be carefully selected, taking into account their interaction with each other, side effects, and range of efficiency.

While your body chemistry has a lot to do with how well you will respond to medical maintenance, your assiduousness in following the course of treatment is also crucial. Most people will take a pill that stops pain or discomfort, but it takes willpower to remember to take one for a condition (blood pressure, high cholesterol) that has no overt symptoms. The willingness to make important life-style changes, such as eating a healthier diet and exercising more, also represents an indispensable part of the therapy. (For more information on life-style changes, see Chapter Nine.)

There are four main classes of medication used to treat coronary artery disease and the associated pain of angina. These are nitrates, beta blockers, calcium antagonists, and anticlotting agents. Additional medications may be given to minimize the coronary risk factors of high serum cholesterol and high blood pressure.

Nitrates

The nitrate compound nitroglycerin has been part of the medical arsenal against angina pains for the past 150 years. It acts to immediately alleviate pain by dilating the coronary arteries. At the same time, it causes veins throughout the body and particularly in the lower limbs to dilate, easing the heart's workload. Because of the pooling of blood in the lower extremities, patients are advised to take the drug while sitting down. If the patient is standing, faintness or dizziness may occur as a result of the drop in blood pressure; the drug is less effective if the patient is lying down.

Nitroglycerin should relieve angina pain within one or two minutes. If the pain continues, take another tablet after five minutes. Nitroglycerin relieves angina pains but not that of a heart attack, so if you do not feel relief after the second tablet you should seek emergency medical treatment.

Nitroglycerin comes in several forms. The most familiar is the tiny white tablet that is placed under the tongue. Longer-acting forms include a tablet that needs to be kept between the upper lip and gum for several hours, an oral/nasal spray, and a small disklike patch containing an ointment that is absorbed through the skin. Nitroglycerin loses its potency with age and exposure to heat, light, or moisture. Since it generally causes a brief, sharp tingling sensation in the scalp and under the tongue, you can easily test your supply to see whether it needs replacing.

Side effects are minimal, the main complaint being short-term headaches (from dilation of arteries in the scalp). Caution should be exercised if you are concurrently taking calcium antagonists—which also dilate the arteries—since the combination can lower your blood pressure sufficiently to cause fainting. If you have glaucoma, you may be advised to cut back on nitroglycerin, as its prolonged use can raise intraocular pressure.

Beta Blockers

One of the greatest boons to the world's heart patients was the discovery of beta blockers, a family of medications that relieve angina, lower blood pressure, prevent cardiac arrhythmias, and may help prevent heart attacks. They have the additional benefits of decreasing the incidence of angina and of lowering blood pressure.

Beta blockers work by occupying some of the receptor sites for the so-called stress hormones (catecholamines) adrenaline and noradrenaline. Adrenaline and noradrenaline are the hormones responsible for our fight-or-flight response. They increase the force with which the heart expels blood, speed up the heart rate, and elevate blood pressure. During a heart attack, massive amounts of noradrenaline pour into the heart muscle, often causing fatal ventricular fibrillation. At the same time, adrenaline increases the heart rate and blood pressure, thus raising the demand for oxygenated blood and more rapidly depleting the already limited supply.

By blocking the receptor sites, beta blockers stop the process before it gets under way. Their usefulness extends beyond the very important function of reducing the likelihood of heart attacks to that of maintaining the heart rate and blood pressure at acceptable levels. They also greatly mitigate the discomfort of angina by lessening the frequency of ischemic episodes and raising the amount of exertion possible before ischemia occurs.

There are currently eight beta blockers available in the U.S. They all perform their good work by the same means, but the dosage required, length of duration in the body, and side effects may vary. One of the oldest and most commonly prescribed beta blockers is propranolol (brand name Inderal), which also comes in a longer-acting, one-a-day form.

Side effects occur in only about five to ten percent of patients taking beta blockers, and these can usually be adequately responded to by changing the brand or dosage. Among the known side effects are cold hands and feet, bronchial difficulty in patients with emphysema or asthma, vivid dreams (when using propranolol), mild muscle weakness or fatigue, depression and reduced libido and impotence. Again, these symptoms are uncommon and can usually be treated without the need for you to stop using these invaluable medications.

Beta blockers should never be discontinued abruptly, or a rebound in chest pain can occur. If you must stop using them, have your cardiologist provide you with a schedule for tapered withdrawal.

Calcium Antagonists

Calcium antagonists first came into use as a palliation for angina around the beginning of the nineteen eighties, and have substantially boosted the viability of medical maintenance for many angina sufferers. The calcium antagonists—also known as calcium blockers, and calcium channel blockers—lower high blood pressure and seem particularly effective in treating the coronary artery spasms of Prinzmetal's angina. They may also prove invaluable in lessening the frequency of silent bouts of ischemia.

These medications function by blocking the channels through which calcium—which is necessary for muscular contraction—is absorbed into the heart muscle and arterial walls. They thus keep the heart relaxed and the arteries dilated.

The calcium antagonists currently approved for use are nifedipine, verapamil, and diltiazem. Nifedipine is the most powerful vasodilator of the three, and it can be safely used in combination with beta blockers. The other two calcium blockers slow the heartbeat down (unlike nifedipine) and can therefore replace beta blockers for patients who react adversely to them.

Side effects occur in less than five percent of patients, and are due to the vessel-dilating properties of the medication. Nifedipine is unusual in occasionally resulting in fluid buildup in the legs (edema), which can usually be corrected with diuretics. Care must be taken in combining calcium antagonists with other blood pressure medication or nitroglycerin so as to avoid too precipitous a drop in blood pressure.

Anticlotting Agents

Blood clots are the nemesis of coronary artery disease patients. They can rapidly transform a narrow artery to a blocked one or break off from a section of atherotic plaque and travel along an artery to block it at a point farther along. Clearly, a medication that will either prevent blood clots from forming or limit their size could prove to be a lifesaver.

In earlier years, anticoagulants, such as warfarin, were prescribed in the hope they would impede clot formation. However, small doses of anticoagulants were not determined to be very effectual, and larger doses or more powerful anticoagulants are impractical because of the risk of uncontrolled or spontaneous bleeding.

Small doses of aspirin, one of the most common medicines available to man, were recently proven useful as a preventive measure against blood clots. Aspirin hinders the clumping of platelets (the sticky, disklike cells that are the body's first defense against bleeding) by blocking an enzyme needed for the formation of platelet adhesion. A very low dose of aspirin—a half a tablet or one "baby" aspirin—is all that is needed, and the beneficial effects are little enhanced by taking more aspirin. (High doses of aspirin may actually be deleterious to the arteries by blocking the formation of prostaglandins, hormones that help protect the arterial wall.)

Aspirin is sometimes prescribed in combination with dipyridamole, a drug that is a potent blocker of platelet clumping in the presence of aspirin.

Cholesterol Reduction

While the optimal means of lessening one's serum cholesterol levels is through a change of diet, medication may be needed to bring down dangerously high levels or for maintaining acceptable levels in people with familial hypercholesterolemia. The medications most commonly used to reduce cholesterol include cholestyramine, clofibrate, nicotinic acid, gemfibrozil, and lovastatin. (These are the generic names; brand names may be different.)

Cholestyramine (and a similar compound, colestipol) are "bile acid sequestrants." They work by binding bile salts in the intestine, the liver's response to which is converting cholesterol into bile acids, which are subsequently excreted. Possible side effects include nausea, bloating, gas, and poor absorption of fat-soluble vitamins (A and D). Cholestyramine usually goes by the brand name Questran, colestipol by Colestid.

High doses of nicotinic acid (also known as niacin), have been shown to be useful in lowering overall cholesterol levels in some people. It may be most useful in conjunction with one or more of the medications listed above. Side effects include a harmless burning facial flush, stomach pain, palpitations, and raised blood sugar in diabetics. Although niacin is available without prescription, you should most definitely not take it without first consulting your physician.

Clofibrate (*Atromid-S*) can lower triglycerides by up to thirty percent and total cholesterol from five to ten percent. It is less frequently prescribed today because of the advent of equally effective drugs with fewer side effects (see gemfibrozil). Potential side effects may include stomach upset, flulike symptoms, nausea, impotence, pancreatitis, and gall-bladder problems.

Gemfibrozil (lopid) causes a significant decrease in triglycerides, some lowering of overall cholesterol levels, and an increase in HDL. Side effects are relatively uncommon, but may include bloating, stomach pain, and nausea.

Lovastatin (earlier called mevinolin) is a recent arrival on the scene (1987), and it may prove the most useful cholesterol-reducing drug, since it is highly potent while having minimal side effects. Lovastatin increases the number of LDL receptors, as well as further lowering cholesterol by interfering with an enzyme, HMG-CoA-Reductase, involved in its formation in the liver. Lovastatin appears to be even more effective if combined with another cholesterol-reducing drug, colestipol.

Blood Pressure Medication

Since several of the drugs normally recommended for angina also lower blood pressure, the medical approach to high blood pressure in coronary artery disease patients may differ from that for people with other conditions or hypertension unaccompanied by other forms of cardiovascular disease. For example, ACE inhibitors are regularly given to lower blood pressure but are not effective against angina. Physicians prefer not to use more than one drug to lower blood pressure. Occasionally, a diuretic (such as one of the class of drugs called thiazides) may be prescribed to bring high blood pressure within the normal range.

Alternative Noninvasive Procedures

When a drain gets clogged, one method of clearing it is to insert a flexible wire and try to dislodge the sludge that has accumulated on the pipe's sides. The idea of doing something similar to unclog coronary arteries occurred to physicians some time ago, and two of today's noninvasive surgical procedures work on this principle. The first, percutaneous transluminal coronary angioplasty, is becoming an increasingly widespread procedure with an ever-improving safety record. The second, laser recanalization, is still highly experimental and is *not* likely to be offered to you as an option by your physician, at least at this time.

Juanita, a fifty-six-year-old medical secretary, during a routine physical examination, learned that there was an abnormality in her ECG. A subsequent stress test was positive, and she agreed to an angiogram, since she was quite concerned about the potential life-threatening implications of silent heart disease. The angiogram revealed a very tight blockage in her right coronary artery, while her left coronary system and left ventricle functioned normally.

Juanita agreed to angioplasty. A week later, she was admitted to the hospital where, during a twenty-minute local anesthesia procedure, the angioplasty was successfully completed. Juanita subsequently returned to work, and has had two normal follow-up stress tests. In addition, she has changed her diet, lost fifteen pounds, and started to exercise regularly in the hopes of preventing further lesions in her coronary arteries.

Percutaneous transluminal coronary angioplasty is usually referred to in medicine by its acronym, PTCA, and by the public as simply angioplasty or balloon angioplasty. In this procedure, which is performed under continuous X-ray fluoroscopy, a balloon catheter is inserted into the femoral or brachial artery and threaded up to the site of the occlusion in the coronary arteries. Up to this point, the operation is identical with the cardiac catheterization performed for a coronary angiogram (the diagnostic test described in Chapter 4). When the tip of the catheter is in place at the site of the atheroma, the balloon is inflated to crush the fatty plaque and push it outward. The balloon may be inflated and deflated several times to crush the plaque more effectively. With the balloon deflated, dye is injected through the catheter to visualize the artery. The physician is thus able to ensure that the size of the blockage has been reduced and a wider channel has been created through which blood can pass more easily. (See diagram.)

When the physician is satisfied that the atheroma has been effectively diminished, the catheter is removed. The patient remains in the coronary care unit for another twenty-four to forty-eight hours, and is carefully

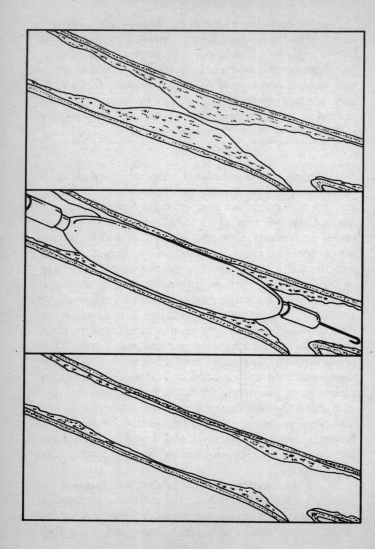

monitored for any electrical disturbances of the heart or ischemic episodes that would indicate a blockage.

Angioplasty is an extremely useful adjunct to the nonsurgical treatment of angina sufferers. There is little physical discomfort for the patient (aside from transient chest pain when the balloon is inflated), no scars or large incisions to worry about, the hospital stay is only three days in the majority of cases, and full recovery is rapid (seven to fourteen days). In about ninety percent of the patients, blood flow through the affected artery is initially significantly improved and angina is alleviated.

The complication rate for angioplasty is higher than that of bypass surgery, however. Approximately three to five percent of patients require emergency coronary bypass surgery, and another five percent suffer heart attacks within twenty-four hours of the operation. Heart attacks occur because the crushing of the plaque can cause debris to break off and clog an artery, and the release of chemicals and cells from the crushing of the plaque can support clotting. Restenosing (stricture) of the artery occurs within a year in close to a third of the anterior dilates (the cases in which the site of the obstruction is not easily reached), requiring either a second angioplasty or bypass surgery. In addition, the operation is quite costly because a surgical team and operating room have to be kept available on standby in the event of an emergency complication.

Balloon angioplasty is an excellent remedy for a carefully selected group of patients. The ideal candidate has a single blocked artery—generally the left anterior or right coronary artery. This should be a recent development, preferably, since angioplasty does not work as well on atheromas that have calcified.

Angioplasty is by no means ruled out for patients

with multiple-vessel disease. As the available technology and the technical skills of physicians performing angioplasty have steadily improved, the patient profile has been changing to include more people with mild forms of multiple-vessel disease. The complication rate of angioplasty has also been steadily improving, and the number of procedures performed goes up every year. In 1986, 133,000 angioplasties were performed, and it is projected that over 200,000 will be conducted in 1990.

It should be emphasized that angioplasty is nevertheless not competitive with coronary bypass surgery and is not suitable for all angina patients. For the right candidates, however, and in the hands of an experienced cardiologist, the procedure offers excellent benefits and a very high success rate.

The use of lasers to burn away fatty plaque in the arteries is currently being examined experimentally. The laser is passed up a catheter that has previously been inserted and guided into place, and the laser is selectively "fired" at the atheromas, effectively melting them away. Animal experiments have found that laser canalization can effectively unblock atherosclerotic arteries in the heart; however, in humans this technique has thus far been used principally to clear away deposits in the arteries of the lower limbs. The main impediment still to be overcome is the risk of injuring or perforating the artery, which has potentially fatal consequences. The additional questions are what happens to the vaporized material as it enters the bloodstream, and how to prevent clots and scar tissue from forming on arterial walls that have suffered insult from the laser. Nevertheless, there is hope that this technique will be made substantially safer before too long, and there is a good chance laser surgery will replace or augment balloon angioplasty within a few years.

CHAPTER 9

Life-style Changes for
a Healthier Heart

The bypass operation can give the coronary artery disease sufferer an almost miraculous extra lease on life. Angina pain often completely subsides, and many patients find they have more energy than they have had in years. However, it should be remembered that the operation is a palliative measure, not a cure. You might liken it to bailing out the water from a boat that has a slow leak. The boat will stay afloat much longer, but it will gradually fill up again unless the leak is stopped. Similarly, the life-style factors that lead to atherosclerotic arteries need to be taken care of in order for the new conduits not to become blocked themselves.

But this is well within your means. You can keep yourself feeling healthier and ensure that your new, bypassing blood vessels stay clear by taking these straightforward measures: eat a low-fat, low-sodium diet; exercise regularly; take medications conscientiously according to the schedule laid out by your cardiologist; reduce stress; and quit smoking. Gone about the right way, these changes can not only be healthful, they can be pleasurable as well. The changes you make in your way of life should be viewed not as a form of punishment or self-denial, but as a means of applying what we know about health in order to live more fully.

Joe, L. a 310-pound advertising executive who had recently undergone bypass surgery, was distressed by the dietary changes urged by his cardiologist. Joe's hobby and greatest pleasure in life was cooking and, of course, eating. Much of his social life, in fact, involved having friends come over to try his latest gourmet creations.

Instead of despairing, giving up his hobby, or reverting to a diet that would without doubt land him back in the hospital, Joe decided to be innovative within these limitations. He soon learned that his guests were just as happy with a dinner of, say, linguine with fresh tomatoes, clams, and green beans (a high-carbohydrate, low-fat meal) as they had been with his celebrated meat dishes with cream sauces. He also found that a range of new cooking styles and cookbooks were opened up to him—today's health awareness having spawned a nouvelle cuisine that reduces fats while emphasizing flavor.

There is a tendency to think of a "diet" as a form of nutritional shock treatment. An eating program is not considered a "real" diet unless it is bland, hard to chew, and shaves the pounds off visibly every other day. The psychological appeal of this sort of diet is that you can tally your progress by how rapidly the scale shifts downward. And since the diet makes you miserable, it must be good for you. Never mind that those pounds (much of which may in fact be liquid) will be back within a few months, that you may have upset the mechanisms that let you know when you are hungry and when you have eaten enough, and that these up-and-down swings are wearing on your body in general.

Perhaps, as is already beginning to happen, we should do away with the concept of a diet altogether and think instead of a lifelong move to a wiser eating pattern. As Joe L. discovered, food does not have to be fatty or salty to taste good. There are an increasing number of first-rate cookbooks that focus on a gourmet cuisine that is healthy for your heart. (Some examples: Jane Brody's *Good Food Book*, Michael DeBakey's *The Living Heart Diet*.) These books are an excellent start, and you will find that as you learn more about healthful cooking you can revamp your own favorite recipes to get rid of their fat or cholesterol-containing elements.

This is important not only when you eat at home but when you dine out as well. There is no need to give up the pleasure of eating in restaurants, but nor should you allow such meals to be nutritional disaster areas. While it is harder to control what goes on in a restaurant kitchen, you can request that your dinner be cooked with less salt or without cream and butter. A good place to start is at the beginning of a meal where bread is served; either eat it plain (its surprising how tasty a choice bread can be on its own) or request margarine instead of butter. You can also try learning more beforehand about the kind of food a restaurant serves, and you can help ensure that your meal is healthful by being careful in what you select (for example, ordering broiled salmon instead of a steak). Restaurateurs are also becoming more aware of their customers' interest in good nutritional habits, and some restaurants feature meals approved by the American Heart Association. If you have doubts about a particular dish, ask the waiter or the maître d'. They will be happy to tell you how the food is cooked and to ask the chef to make any changes or substitutions that you suggest.

The main changes you will need to make as part of a sound nutrition program are cutting down (or cutting out) animal fats and cholesterol-rich foods (such as red meat), lowering your sodium intake, and consuming more foods containing complex carbohydrates and fiber. A maxim to remember for any diet: Because some is beneficial, it does not follow that a lot of it is good for you. Balance is really the key element to sound nutrition, and your daily intake should include fruits, vegetables, whole-grain cereals or breads, and complex carbohydrates (pasta, potatoes, beans) along with small amounts of high protein foods such as meat, poultry, dairy products, eggs, and fish (which can safely be eaten in larger quantities provided it is cooked with little fat).

If you have high blood cholesterol, it is vital that you lower it. To do this, you should minimize your intake of saturated fats, especially those in whole milk, cream, butter, red meat or organs (such as liver), eggs, bacon, and other foods containing or cooked in animal fats. Monounsaturated oils, such as olive oil, and polyunsaturated oils, such as corn or safflower oils, should be substituted for saturated fats (lard, butter, coconut or palm oil) wherever possible . . . something that is usually easy to do when cooking.

The American Heart Association recommends that a maximum of thirty percent of one's daily calorie intake should come from fat. No more than ten percent of this should come from saturated fats, ten percent from polyunsaturated fats, and the rest from monounsaturated fats. Currently, the average American consumes a diet in which forty percent of the calories come from fat and close to half of this from saturated fats. The AHA also recommends that dietary cholesterol consumption be limited to 300 milligrams per day, and preferably less. (Egg yolks contain approximately 225 milligrams, hence the AHA recommends not eating more than two egg yolks per week.)

Table salt and foods containing sodium (canned soups and vegetables are often very high in salt, as are bottled sauces) should be cut down as part of a program to lower blood pressure. Salt does not "cause" hypertension, which is usually the result of some unknown inherited tendency. However, lowering the salt intake helps to stem existing high blood pressure. The reason for this is that salt and water accumulate in the kidneys and change the tone of the arterial walls, causing them to constrict. The Western diet, which is high in salt, has habituated us to using far more than we need to give food flavor. If you cut down on salt, food may taste bland for a while until you get used to it, but you *can* rehabituate yourself to enjoy foods that contain very little salt. One way to add to the flavor is to be more creative with spices and fresh herbs.

Complex carbohydrates are found in such foods as potatoes, pasta, and whole grains. They are not only low in fat and high in fiber, but they also contribute essential vitamins and minerals as well as protein. At one time, potatoes and pasta were thought of as fattening. The culprits, however, were what we put *on* these foods: gobs of cheese, sour cream, cream sauces, and butter. Today, most nutritionists agree that the majority of one's calories should be consumed in the form of complex carbohydrates. A high-carbohydrate diet not only helps lower serum cholesterol levels, it also helps control diabetes and may lessen the risk of some cancers.

Fiber is an important part of our diet, although it is indigestible and does not provide us with any nutrients. Soluble fiber—which includes oat bran, gums (such as guar), and pectin from fruits and legumes (beans, lentils, et cetera)—appears actually to decrease serum cholesterol levels. This is probably due to its binding to bile salts in the stomach and small bowel, and thus encouraging the liver to convert cholesterol into bile acids which would be subsequently excreted. Insoluble fiber, found in the cell walls of plants (*cellulose*) and in the husks of whole grains (*hemicellulose*), helps to provide bulk to the stool and speed its progress through the bowels.

Oat bran has gotten a great deal of media attention and advertising lately and is indeed an excellent source of fiber. Consumers should be warned, however, that store-bought oat bran products such as muffins can contain a fair amount of sugar and fats and very little oat bran. A recent *New York Times* survey found many commercial muffins to range anywhere from four hundred to seven hundred calories each. Again, balance is important, and you should not forget that there are many other valuable sources of fiber as well. A stalk of celery or a raw carrot, for example, can provide a pleasant snack that is high in fiber. Fiber pills, however, are frowned on by most nutrition experts. Such pills do not encourage better eating habits, are of limited digestive value, and can sometimes cause gastric distress.

While sugar has not been proven to accelerate atherosclerosis, candy and sweet desserts should nevertheless be kept down to a minimum. Refined sugar provides calories but no other nutrients. The occasional cookie or candy is acceptable, but moderation is in the best interest of health promotion.

Changes in the *way* you eat can assist in providing better nutrition and supporting weight reduction. People who overeat also often eat too quickly. Try to slow down and savor your food, or try taking breaks between courses. Skipping breakfast and/or lunch backfires because you will become so hungry that you are likely to overeat later in the day. Between-meal snacks should either be cut out altogether or planned in advance to ensure they are low-fat, nutritious, and part of your day's total calorie plan. Sometimes people who strictly observe a nutrition program during each meal will ruin their good work by eating such high-sodium, high-fat snacks as salted nuts during their leisure moments.

Staying aware of what foods you consume is part of any good dietary regimen. It can be helpful to read labels in the supermarket closely. Advertisers have discovered the buzz words *low-* (or *reduced-*) *cholesterol* and *high-fiber* and sprinkle such phrases liberally on packages containing food that might also be high in sodium, sugar, and fats, including the highly saturated tropical oils (palm, palm kernel, and coconut).

We do not have the scope in this book to provide you with all the nutrition information you might need, or with appropriate recipes. We do recommend, however, that you follow the guidelines suggested by your hospital as well as continuing to learn more about nutrition on your own. It is within everyone's reach to maintain a diet that is appetizing, nutritious, and low in fat.

*   *   *

"The wise, for cure, on exercise depend," wrote the noted British poet John Dryden in the year 1700. Indeed, the value of exercise in promoting good health was recognized more than twenty-two centuries ago by Hippocrates, and is being ever more strongly urged by medical associations and presidential commissions today. Exercise benefits the body's overall health, and that of the heart in particular. Cardiovascular output and general muscle tone are enhanced by regular exercise, and the blood levels of HDL (the "good" cholesterol) may be raised while that of LDL and triglycerides are decreased. You will also have an increased feeling of well-being and may be more resistant to infection.

The kinds of exercise to engage in and the recommended amount pose special considerations for all heart patients. Your cardiologist will give you appropriate guidelines, and should be consulted before beginning any new exercise regimen. While you can get adequate exercise on your own with simple, inexpensive equipment —for example, a pair of properly fitted walking shoes— you may also wish to ask your cardiologist about special exercise training programs for cardiac patients. Some people find they prefer the discipline of exercising with a regular group that offers companionship as well as incentive.

Among the most beneficial exercises for heart health are walking, jogging, bicycling, swimming, rowing, and cross-country skiing (on a machine or in the snow). All of these require very little outlay in the way of equipment, minimal training, and can be tailored to suit your needs and fitness level. You should decide which of these, or any combination, you most enjoy and see to it that you do the exercise at least three to four times a week. You may find that setting a particular time of day every day to exercise will keep you on your schedule—for example, riding a stationary bicycle while you watch the evening news.

There are several things to remember about any aerobic exercise that will both help you keep doing it and avoid injury or muscle strain. Start your program out slowly, and do less initially than you feel you are capable of doing. During the course of exercise it is possible to overstrain a muscle without realizing that you are doing so, because your adrenaline is up and endorphins—the body's chemical painkillers—are blocking the awareness of pain. If you feel stiff the day after, this is a signal to warm up more and to reduce the amount of exercise. As your muscle tone builds, you can gradually exercise harder and for longer duration.

"Warming up" means doing very light exercise—jogging on the spot very slowly—for a few minutes. Always warm up before exercising. This decreases the strain on your heart and on your muscles. Stretch your muscles *after* warming up. Don't "bounce" or try to stretch farther than is comfortable, but rather hold a stretch position for a minute or two.

Cool down after exercising by doing the same activity at a slower pace for a few moments. Stopping suddenly after exercising puts strain on your heart, since the muscles of your limbs are still crying out for oxygenated blood but are no longer helping to distribute it. This can cause a drop in the supply of blood to the heart and the brain. Also, avoid exercising immediately after eating. Blood pools in your stomach to aid with digestion, and exercising would require your heart to work harder than normal to achieve adequate circulation.

Some forms of exercise you should avoid altogether or only attempt under the strict supervision of your cardiologist. Weight training and other isometric exercises can be dangerous to anyone with cardiovascular disorders. The act of lifting weights increases blood pressure and can put considerable strain on the heart. If you feel strongly about building muscular strength, ask your cardiologist to lay out a program for you using Heavyhands, small hand-held weights that let you combine aerobic and isometric activity.

A final word of advice: Do the exercise you enjoy most, don't overdo it, and make sure that you keep it up.

After the bypass operation, your cardiologist may want you to continue to take medication to cut down cholesterol, ease the workload of your heart, and lower your blood pressure. (For more about these medications, see Chapter Eight.) Your doctor will prescribe a schedule of medications and will increase or reduce them according to how your health progresses and how you react to the particular drugs. You should not make any changes in this regimen without first consulting with your cardiologist. Studies of how closely patients follow the guidelines for medication taken at home have established that there is some tendency for people to take their medication when they're feeling symptoms and stop taking it when they feel better. This is a mistake. Do not stop taking medication, increase the dosage, or substitute other drugs except on the advice of your doctor!

This is not to say that you should suffer side effects in silence. Inform your physician of any adverse effects of the drugs and ask him or her to suggest an adjusted dosage or an alternative. You should also check with your doctor's office before taking any over-the-counter medications, and if you are seeing any doctors for other unrelated conditions you should inform them as to which medications you are currently taking.

Many studies found that a daily dose of aspirin is effective in reducing the risk of heart attacks. Small doses of aspirin prevent blood clots from forming by blocking an enzyme within the blood platelets, and, used in conjunction with dipyridamole, appears to prevent clots in bypass patients' vein grafts. Aspirin is not recommended for people who suffer from peptic ulcers and other conditions where there is a risk of internal bleeding. Aspirin does not actually cause bleeding, but it does slow down the blood's clotting ability. Some people find that aspirin irritates their stomach, but this side effect can usually be alleviated by switching to a coated brand of aspirin—but not another analgesic, such as Tylenol or ibuprofen, which are different compounds altogether! Check with your cardiologist whether you should be taking aspirin and what the dose should be.

Stress is another risk factor that has an impact on overall health, as well as the cardiovascular system. Our physical response to stress—including raised hormone and adrenaline levels, increased heartbeat, slowed-down kidney function—was originally a protective reaction to impending danger. In threatening situations, it allows us to marshal all our physical resources toward a quick attack or escape, and therefore is known as the "fight-or-flight" response. This same reaction without outlet over a long period has deleterious effects on the body.

The good news is that the amount of stress we experience can be lessened. Remember, day-to-day stress is not occasioned by the amount of work there is to be done but by feelings of a lack of control or of hostility. While one cannot expect people to change their personalities at will, relaxation techniques can go a long way in cutting back on everyday stress.

There are several ways of making relaxation part of your daily program. One is to set aside a certain amount of time to do something you enjoy, such as reading novels or poetry or listening to music. Make sure that this time is wholly your own and that you will not be interrupted—if you expect the phone to ring at any moment, you will not be able to relax fully.

Deep-breathing exercises, meditation, and meditative "exercise" such as yoga and t'ai chi can help you relax, while taking relatively little of your time. Virtually all non-Western medicine makes use of trancelike states of deep relaxation to respond to poor health, and Western physicians are coming around to the viewpoint that these can be a useful adjunct to a medically oriented course of treatment. To learn more about relaxation techniques, you may wish to take a course at your local community college, university extension, or YMCA.

Unavoidable life stresses—such as the death of a family member or a close friend—can also be coped with more effectively if the feelings of grief or helplessness are expressed and shared. Support groups and counseling are recommended for helping to deal with loss and other profound sources of stress.

If you have recently suffered a personal loss, are distressed by having retired early, or are prevented from doing formerly favorite activities by a physical disability, you may find a support group helpful as a way to share and resolve your feelings. Women—who outlive men by about ten years on average—not only often have better social networks to discuss and share personal crises with but are more inclined to join formalized support groups. Too many men still see such groups as a last resort.

Our culture has tended to socialize men to internalize stress by discouraging them from expressing feelings of weakness, fear, or other strong emotions. *Be stoical. Never admit that things seem too much for you. And, above all, never cry.* These are the unspoken (and occasionally spoken) messages ingrained into males from early childhood. These codes of behavior may be useful on the playing field or in the boardroom, but they're hard on the arteries. The ability to share our weaknesses as well as our strengths is part of what makes us human, and our society is finally beginning to recognize that it's perfectly okay for men to express their emotions openly. In fact, it's much healthier.

To find out about support groups in your area, check with your physician, a religious advisor (such as a rabbi or priest), or a local branch of the American Heart Association or the American Psychiatric Association.

BREAKING BAD HABITS

Smoking

No discussion of life-style modification can be complete without talking about the effects of tobacco, alcohol, and illicit drugs. As emphasized earlier, cigarette smoking is a major risk factor for a heart attack, and stopping smoking is probably the single most important step you can take to improve heart health. This is particularly important for bypass patients; in fact, some leading heart surgeons refuse to do a coronary bypass in a patient who smokes until he or she has stopped.

As any smoker knows, quitting is easier said than done. Nicotine is highly addictive; in fact, Dr. C. Everett Koop, the former Surgeon General and an outspoken foe of tobacco use, stressed that it is just as addictive as cocaine. By definition, overcoming an addiction means encountering withdrawal symptoms as the body adjusts to cessation of the addictive substance. For cigarette smokers, these symptoms range from mild to severe. The most common are feelings of nervousness, anxiety, headache, and difficulty sleeping, sitting still, or concentrating. These may be intense for a few days to a week or two.

There are numerous ways to go about stopping smoking. Quitting abruptly (cold turkey) remains the most common—about ninety-five percent of ex-smokers used this method. It also should be noted that some ninety percent of ex-smokers resumed the habit one or more times before succeeding in quitting for good; thus, backsliding should not be considered a sign of failure.

There also are numerous sources of help for people who want to stop smoking. These include self-help groups, such as those sponsored by the American Heart Association, American Cancer Society, Seventh Day Adventist church, employers, and other organizations. Commercial stop-smoking programs such as Smokenders work well for some people. Self-hypnosis has also helped many smokers quit.

At least two prescription products can help ease withdrawal symptoms. The most widely used is nicotine gum. This is chewed for several weeks during the quitting phase to avoid nicotine-withdrawal symptoms, and then once you are accustomed to not smoking, the gum is gradually withdrawn. Researchers at Columbia University have found that taking clonidine—a prescription drug normally used to treat high blood pressure—also can ease withdrawal symptoms. The drug is given for a week or two before stopping and continued for about three weeks after quitting. If you are having problems stopping smoking, by all means talk to your doctor.

Alcohol Use

Many people have the notion that a drink or two is actually good for the heart. This idea originated in studies showing that moderate amounts of alcohol can produce a modest increase in HDL levels. Other studies have found, however, that even a small amount of alcohol consumed regularly increases the risk of a stroke. And drinking more than an ounce or so of liquor (or the equivalent amount in wine or beer) damages the heart and blood vessels. Alcoholics often develop heart-muscle disease (alcohol-related cardiomyopathy), which leads to congestive heart failure. An occasional drink or a glass of wine with dinner probably does no harm, but consistent drinking of more than that should be avoided, especially if you already have heart disease.

Illicit Drug Use

A number of illicit drugs, especially cocaine and its derivatives, have a dangerous effect on the heart. The rash of sudden deaths among prominent athletes has helped raise public awareness of the dangers of cocaine to the heart. Studies indicate that the cardiovascular effects of smoking marijuana are comparable to, or even worse than, tobacco use. Street drugs also can damage the heart. Everyone should steer clear of illicit drugs, but this is especially true of heart patients. If you have a substance-abuse problem, seek help in overcoming it.

CHAPTER 10

Making Decisions: Dealing with Doctors and the Hospital

The choice of whether or not to have coronary artery bypass surgery is clearly a momentous one. It's hard to imagine another decision that will have such an impact on your health and life-style, as well as such a disruption in the short term. Your doctor can supply you with the medical reasons for undergoing surgery and may strongly urge you in that direction, but the decision is ultimately your own. You are the final arbiter of what happens to your own body.

For this reason it's important that you work with your doctor to arrive at the best medical course of action for you. Your attitude should not be merely "Whatever my doctor says is fine with me." Seeing a doctor does not mean you can simply place your medical fate in another person's hands. Rather, taking an active role in determining your own treatment will greatly benefit your health.

And your active role begins by your becoming informed, both about your own condition and about the surgery itself. Much of the anxiety raised by any major operation in large part derives from a fear of the unknown. Once you have access to information as to what the surgery entails and what you need to expect, the prospect is bound to feel far less scary and the discomforts far easier to endure. Also, what many surgical patients find most vexing is a sense of lost control (indeed, this is often a source of desperation or anger). Knowing what is going on and how to address the issues steers you from a helpless to an empowered role. And finally, someone who is knowledgeable about the operation is in a much better position to make the best decision and ask the right questions about their own circumstances. Before agreeing to any major surgery, you should make sure that you understand exactly why you need the operation, what benefits and possible complications it presents, and what alternatives are out there.

Knowing that you are ill and may require an operation is undoubtedly a frightening experience, one that can strike at the very root of a person's sense of self-worth. (Think of the judgmental phrases we often use to describe illness: "There's something wrong with me." "I'm not what I used to be.") People sometimes react to this state by going to extremes: the patient who wants to know nothing of his treatment and who passively gives himself up to the medical establishment ("Wake me up when the operation's over. . . .") versus the patient who regards every suggestion made by a medical professional with the utmost suspicion, and who seeks to control every facet of the treatment down to selecting the nurses and ancillary staff.

The ideal patient (both from the physician's point of view and in terms of getting the maximum value from our way of medicine) is one who lies somewhere in the middle of these polar opposites. This patient is interested in learning more about his or her illness and what can be done about it, is open to the physician's suggestions (which are, after all, based on expertise and knowledge), but is also willing to express his or her fears, health goals, and personal needs.

The doctor charged with your care both prior to the operation and in the all-important recovery phase is the cardiologist, a specialist in the function of the heart and its diseases. (Even if your general practitioner is the person who first detects the possibility that you have coronary artery disease, he or she will usually refer you to a cardiologist.) Your cardiologist's recommendation will obviously carry much weight in your ultimate decision, so it is vital that you have a doctor whom you're comfortable with and who you feel is responsive to your own questions and concerns.

As your relationship with your cardiologist will hopefully be a good one, care in the initial choice can save you unhappiness later on. When looking for a cardiologist, you can seek the recommendation of friends and/or a family physician, or you can contact a local hospital or research center. The cardiologist should be board certified in internal medicine and cardiology and have admitting privileges at a reputable hospital. You may want to meet with the doctor before settling on his or her care. It's important that this is someone you feel you can have a dialogue with and that he or she clearly understands your needs as both a person and a patient. Although you'd want to avoid this by making a careful choice at the outset, if at any point your relationship with your doctor proves unsatisfactory, you can of course switch.

The patient-doctor relationship needs to be a two-way street. While it is your doctor's duty to keep you well informed, the reverse is also true. Your own willingness to keep him or her up to date as to the state of your health can impact how your doctor determines the most productive treatment. If you are being treated for any other health disorder—mental or physical—it is vital that you fully inform your cardiologist (and, later, the cardiothoracic surgeon) about this before you have surgery. Many conditions can make you vulnerable to certain complications or may present additional surgical risks. Similarly, specific medications can cause serious side effects when combined with the medicines you may need in the process of your cardiac treatment. You should also let your doctor know whether you have been diligent in taking any medication that has been prescribed for you, how much alcohol you consume on a regular basis, and whether you use any narcotics or sleeping pills. Don't let embarrassment keep you from getting the most efficacious health care.

Your doctor can best provide you with the information you need if you can clarify exactly what it is you want to know. No doctor is a mind reader, and few can take the time to draw this information out of you. This may sound self-evident, yet many patients are reluctant to voice concerns or appear uninformed. Lots of people are intimidated by physicians, who rush about, always having important business waiting for them. This is understandable, but it's a good idea to remember that your doctor is providing you with a service, and it's up to you to make sure that you get the level of service you deserve. Providing you with relevant information is a part of that service, and you need not feel a "bother" by seeking out that information. On the contrary, a physician will probably be pleased when a patient makes the effort to become informed.

One good way to make sure you cover all the necessary questions is to make a list of them before the office visit. There's no reason to feel silly about doing this. First of all, as you may be nervous during the session this takes away the pressure of having to remember your questions on top of it. Also, it can be the most efficient means in terms of time. Your family, too, can be helpful in coming up with questions, and this may give them an opportunity to mention their own qualms and misgivings.

Some of the commonly asked questions are:

1. How will this procedure help me? Will it relieve me of angina pain and/or extend my life?

2. What are the risks and possible complications?

3. How long will the recovery take? What physical limitations will I face during that period?

4. How long can I expect the benefits to last? Is there anything I can do to enhance this?

5. What is my prognosis if I don't have the operation and try medical maintenance and/or angioplasty instead?

6. Are there any unusual aspects of my condition that could affect the likely success of the operation?

7. How soon should I have the operation? Are there any benefits to either deferring or expediting the surgery?

8. What preparations should I make before the operation? Can I donate blood myself, or should I have a friend or family member make a donation in my name?

In order to help you evaluate your own options we recommend that you review the information in Chapter Four on the standard indications and contraindications for the surgery. You should also feel free to ask your cardiologist how you fit into these patterns, or how your case differs from the norm. Most doctors are perfectly willing to explain the reasoning their conclusions and recommendations are based on, but the questions do have to be raised first. Your doctor is your first and best information source, and he or she will know where to send you—books, magazine articles, specific organizations—for anything else you need to know.

Another step in evaluating the need for coronary artery bypass surgery is to seek a second opinion. This is not merely for cases where the indications are unclear. In fact, most insurance companies insist that a second doctor be called in to confirm the diagnosis before they will pay for any major elective surgery. (Some insurance companies have very specific guidelines as to the most appropriate doctor to provide the second opinion, so you should examine your insurance contract carefully and possibly get in touch with the insurance agent as well.)

The doctor who provides the second opinion will usually be another cardiologist (or, in some instances, a cardiothoracic surgeon). To avoid any possible conflict of interest, the consulting physician should be one who 1) has not been referred by your cardiologist and whose practice is completely separate, and 2) will not be performing the operation. This latter stricture is not always feasible, particularly if you have outlying complications, in which case the recommendation to operate may need to come from the particular surgeon who has had the most experience with similar cases.

In general, the process of getting a second opinion is fairly standard. You arrange for the results of your angiogram and other tests to be sent to the consulting doctor, who will review them. This doctor will also ask you about your case history and family background and conduct a physical examination (often including a stress test). You usually do not need to mention the name of your primary physician until after the consulting doctor has submitted his or her opinion, but you should always be up front about the reasons for your visit. You do not need to feel any embarrassment about seeking a second opinion—most doctors would get one themselves if they were in your position. Also, having another doctor concur with the recommendation will undoubtedly allay any of your doubts and leave you feeling better about the prospect.

If there is a disagreement, however, this can raise some complexities. You may choose to make the decision yourself, based on your own feelings about your condition and your sense of the two physicians involved. You may also choose to get a third opinion. One possible approach here is to consult a university hospital and ask to be put in touch with a specialist in your condition, informing them of the reason for your request. Bypass surgery has made rapid advances in the last few years, and someone who is well versed in the most recent findings may be better able to weigh the pros and cons of your particular case.

One other point about second opinions that is frequently overlooked: Their importance is not limited to those instances where a doctor has advised a patient to have surgery, as the following case study demonstrates.

James R., who was recovering from a recent heart attack, had come into the hospital for an examination and angiogram. While providing the attending physician with his medical history, the sixty-three-year-old former businessman revealed that he had suffered from crippling angina for the past fifteen years. In fact, this had led to his early retirement five years ago, a move which had been emotionally devastating for him, as his career had always held a central position in his life. The physician he had consulted upon having his first episode of angina attacks had suggested a cautious approach to his illness, advising against bypass surgery.

James subsequently had a triple bypass, which successfully revascularized his occluded arteries. After a period of recovery, he reported having more energy and a freedom from chest pain that earlier he would not have believed possible. Had James sought a second opinion years before, it is quite likely that surgery could have prevented his premature retirement, years of pain, and possibly the heart attack that had led him finally to seek more aggressive treatment.

If you feel that your symptoms intrude on your quality of life to an unacceptable degree, or if your physician, who you suspect to be overly cautious and conservative about these matters, dissuades you from undergoing surgery, you may wish to get yet another doctor's point of view. Similarly, if the stated reason for forgoing surgery is not the condition of your coronary arteries, but rather some other factor—such as diabetes, gender, or old age—then consulting a surgeon who specializes in such cases may well be warranted. The reasons a surgeon might turn down a candidate are many and varied (and undoubtedly these can sometimes include a reluctance to mar his or her reputation by taking on an excessive number of high-risk cases), and there are more than a few instances of a patient who has been turned down by one surgeon being successfully operated on by another. In all such cases, the risks of the operation have to be carefully weighed against its benefits. Be sure you fully discuss this issue with your cardiologist and/or heart surgeon.

Settling on *where* to have the surgery performed and by which surgeon or surgical team can be as important as the decision whether to have the surgery or not. This is especially true if you fall into any of the high-risk categories described in Chapter Seven, or you have a complicating condition such as heart-valve disease. Bypass surgery has sometimes been described as a numbers game: the more such operations performed at a particular center, the better qualified the surgical team and the supporting personnel are to deal with any challenges that may occur.

There are several ways to set about finding a suitable surgical team. You can begin by asking for recommendations from your physician or from friends or relatives who have had bypass surgery themselves. If the endorsement of a particular doctor comes from friends or relatives, be warned that the circumstances of their illness may have been different from your own. Just as every heart is unique, so is every case of coronary artery disease. Your quest should be for the surgeon who is right for your distinct situation, and not necessarily the guy who was so nice to Uncle Joe.

If you get a referral from your physician or cardiologist, you may want to ask the following questions:

1. What is your acquaintance with this surgeon? Have you worked with this surgeon personally or do you know him/her by reputation only?
2. Why is this the best surgeon, surgical team, or hospital for my particular condition?
3. Who would you have perform the operation if you were in my shoes?
4. Is he or she easy to talk to and willing to counsel family members?

Further ways to find out about appropriate surgical teams include checking with your local university hospital, a lay group who have had the surgery (the so-called zipper clubs), your county medical society, or the American Heart Association (particularly if you have an unusual condition that could present complications).

Once you have narrowed your choices down to one or two hospitals, you can contact them and request information about the number and type of coronary bypass operations they perform annually. (An appropriate number is around 100 per year or more.) You can also ask to see the quality-assurance statements. Quality assurance is a form of voluntary peer review conducted within most hospitals that belong to the Joint Commission on Accreditation of Hospitals (JCAH). These statements will include data about the number of operations performed, as well as the mortality and complication rates. The layman is cautioned not to try to interpret the raw data too strictly—i.e., some of the country's finest hospitals and surgeons may show a higher mortality rate because they perform a greater number of difficult, high-risk operations. There is no reason, however, why you shouldn't ask for an explanation for high mortality or morbidity (postoperative illness and complications) statistics.

After you have narrowed down your choice to a particular hospital, surgical team, or surgeon, you will finally get to meet the cardiothoracic surgeon who will perform your operation. While the surgeon is obviously a key figure in this whole process, you should bear in mind that you are hiring this person principally for his or her technical skill at the operating table. Surgeons rarely have the time to establish the kind of relationship with a patient that a good cardiologist ideally should. You will in all likelihood not be seeing the surgeon more than three or four times after your hospital discharge. However, you do need to feel comfortable with and confident in the surgeon, and his or her team approach.

Before you commit yourself to a particular surgeon, you may want to ask him or her (or an assistant who can answer on the surgeon's behalf) the following questions:

1. How many bypass operations do you/your surgical team perform each week?

2. How frequently do you operate on people with my particular condition?

3. Do you work regularly with the anesthesiologist and the surgical team who will be performing my operation? (Things are more likely to run smoothly if the whole team, including the anesthesiologist, are used to working as one unit.)

4. Would you be using the internal mammary artery as well as the saphenous veins to create my bypasses?

5. Do you have the ancillary staff at hand to deal with my special needs? (This is important if you are elderly, diabetic, et cetera.)

6. Are you board certified by the American Board of Surgery and the American Board of Thoracic Surgery?

Another issue that can have a bearing on your decision where to have the surgery is the question of cost. The cost of the operation varies from around twenty thousand to thirty thousand dollars. If complications require a lengthier hospital stay, this may increase the overall expense. If the best hospital for you is in another state, transportation and accommodation in hotels for you and your family may further add to your costs.

One way to keep costs down is to check out your insurance policy thoroughly. Some policies will cover almost everything and may even help defray travel costs if deemed a necessary part of the treatment; others will only pay for the operation if it is performed at a designated hospital; and still others may allow you to have surgery anywhere you wish but will have caps on the total outlay for this kind of operation. Forewarned is forearmed, and you should make sure you get the best health care possible within your financial constraints. Do not be embarrassed to ask your insurance agent about your coverage, or to ask the hospital under what circumstances payment on assignment is accepted.

The billing procedure can be complicated and baffling. The last thing the patient who is recovering from surgery wants to deal with is trying to figure out a large and complicated bill. You can ask the hospital to assign someone in their billing office to help you sort out your account. You can often have your insurance company or companies billed directly, saving you the worry of trying to figure out what is covered and what isn't.

A new development that may lead to cost containment currently being looked into is a flat fee system. Some hospitals may offer a single rate for the entire operation, instead of separate bills for hospital expenses, surgeons, and other specialists. Such programs have not yet been widely instituted, and they have been criticized for a number of reasons: that they may limit the patient's right to pick the surgeon of his or her choice, that they could limit the care given to the patient who suffers complications, and that they force doctors to accept a thinly disguised form of "socialized medicine."

Finally, while cost concerns are important, it is vital not to cut corners when it comes to your health. Your decision whether to have coronary artery bypass surgery —and, often, where to have it performed—should be made principally on the basis of the medical merits involved. Strictly financial savings often turn out to be illusory: medical treatment can, in the long run, prove as expensive as surgical treatment, for example. And any financial saving that risks compromising your health should clearly not be considered. Again, this is something you should discuss fully with your surgeon or cardiologist—particularly if you are putting off vital health decisions for financial reasons.

Index